Copyright 2015 Miguel Reynolds
Cover design by Madalena Durão

All rights reserved

No part of this book may be reproduced in any form or by any electronic or mechanical means including information storage and retrieval systems, without permission in writing from the authors. The only exception is by a reviewer, who may quote short excerpts in a review.

ISBN-13:
978-1512206166
ISBN-10:
1512206164

For updates, information, ideas and participation visit:
http://www.thesustainableorganisation.com

TABLE OF CONTENTS

INTRODUCTION — 12

Does power have a positive effect on human relationships? 14
How does one distinguish power from influence? 14

PART I — 20

GLOBAL CONTEXT: WHY CHANGE IS NEEDED — 21

MYTH: Growth benefits everyone, or at least most people. 27
GLOBAL GAP 27
GROSS DOMESTIC PRODUCT (GDP) 33
MYTH: A growing GDP infers economic growth. 33

GROSS NATIONAL PRODUCT (GNP) 36
GINI COEFFICIENT 36
GROSS NATIONAL HAPPINESS (GNH) 39
MEDIAN VERSUS MEAN 41
PALMA RATIO 42
OTHER METRICS 43
THE NEED FOR REGULATION 46
THE POLEMIC DODD-FRANK ACT 48
HARSH CRITICISM 50
US' WHOPPING FIGURES 53
THE FUTURE OF THE DODD-FRANK ACT 54
NORTH AMERICA 59
AUSTRALASIA 60
NEW ZEALAND 61
EUROPE 62
UNITED KINGDOM (UK) 63
SWITZERLAND 64
FRANCE 66
SPAIN 67
PORTUGAL 67
NORWAY 68
SWEDEN 68
SOUTH AFRICA 69
MYTH: CEO compensation is calculated according to the performance of the executive and the company... 70

CHINA 70
BRAZIL 71
MYTH: In the US, the work of top CEOs is more than 200 times more valuable than that of regular company employees 71

JAPAN 72

GLOBAL PROBLEM 73

FRACTIONAL RESERVE 77
THE CAPITAL MARKET 79
CARTELS 79
Do we need promotions? 81

HIGH-SPEED TRADING 81
THE FINANCIAL INDUSTRY IS TO BLAME 85
MYTH: Stocks that go up must come down (and vice versa) 85

IMPACT ON PERFORMANCE 88
MYTH: Employees need to start on a low salary to gain motivation to get to the top. 89

MYTH: Some degree of inequality could benefit corporate performance. 90

GLOBAL SOLUTION 96

MYTH: Money first, happiness later 101

THE MARGINAL MILLION THEORY 105
Does money buy everything? 107

MOOCs 109
PEER-TO-PEER 111
A NEW MONEY MOVEMENT 113
LOCAL CURRENCIES 114
THE FULL CROWDSOURCING ORGANISATION 117
JACK WELSH 119
OTHER INNOVATORS 120
PUTTING PEOPLE FIRST 125
SAS INSTITUTE 126
GOOGLE'S SUCCESS 128

PART II 133

THE SUSTAINABLE ORGANISATION MODEL 134

1 – FROM COMPETITIVENESS TO COOPERATION...........138

A WORLD OF HIERARCHIES..139
DEFYING HIERARCHIES 141
Do we need hierarchy?..141

THE TRUST HORMONE 143
COLLECTIVISM AND HOLOGRAPHY...144
Is greed good?..144

THE RISK OF SCALING UP..146
Can we rely on our capabilities and influence instead of rankings and titles? 146

Can people perform without pressure?..147

COORDINATION PALADINS..147
A CHANGE OF VALUES..149
REINFORCING COOPERATION 150
Do we really need competition?..150

2 – FROM AUTHORITY TO RECOGNITION.......................154

MERCENARIES AND MISSIONARIES 155
THE ROLE OF TRANSPARENCY 157
KNOWLEDGE & INFLUENCE 159
Can't we just trust and be eventually disappointed instead of never be disappointed and never sense trust? 159

RESPECT & RECOGNITION...160
COMMITMENT 162
SUSTAINABILITY PALADINS 163
Should knowledge be free and accessible? 164

THE "NEW ECONOMY" LEADER..165
Is anyone born with a title?...165

3 – FROM UNFAIR WAGES TO FAIR REWARDING 171

PAY IS NOT LINKED TO PERFORMANCE 173
A SUSTAINABLE SYSTEM 175
Merit is a product of Knowledge and Transparency 175

Trust results from Merit and Accountability.......................................176

Trust and Fairness develop Harmony 177
Merit and Harmony promote Mobilisation 178
Strategy, Merit and Harmony create Sustainability! 178
Sustainability empowers Justice, Security and ultimately, Happiness
 179

THE COXSWAIN CEO 180
IMPLEMENTING A FAIRER RATIO 181

4 – FROM STOCK PERFORMANCE TO THE SUSTAINABLE ORGANISATION INDEX 187

Does speculation bring any economic benefit? 188

A CHANGE OF PURPOSE 190
TRUE VALUE 192
THE SUSTAINABLE ORGANISATION INDEX (SORG) 195
APPLYING THE SORG 200
GOING DEEPER IN THE ANALYSIS: BREAKING UP SORG 202
GOING DEEPER IN THE ANALYSIS: LOOKING INSIDE THE ORGANISATION
 203
CONCLUDING THE SORG ANALYSIS 203
THE IMPACT FACTOR 204
EXTREME TYPES OF ORGANISATIONS 208

CONCLUSION 212

ABOUT THE AUTHORS 215

ENDNOTES 216

FOREWORD

It is highly stimulating and challenging to write the foreword of the book "The Sustainable Organization" which in good time the authors Miguel Reynolds and Nádia Morais have decided to publish, requesting the participation of some readers with ideas and suggestions.

To dare to write a book on the issue of the organizational sustainability, however vital and essential it may be, in a historical moment when the own viability of the human civilization on Planet Earth, in the short medium-term (one hundred to three hundred years) is questioned globally as never before in human history, is, as I have already stated, challenging but surely opportune and important.

As a college professor, doctor and humanitarian, who, for the past 40 years, has lived, worked and reflected with and on the worst humanitarian crises of our world, I still believe that the problems we have already faced and those that we will face very soon, in ten to twenty years, have a solution as long as we manage our human sensitivity and intelligence.

The tremendous challenges that now appear as the new "Horsemen of the Apocalypse", have indeed solutions and are an opportunity to rethink what sort of human society we want! Sustainable, that is, with a future, if possible, much better for the generations to come!

There will be no sustainable future if we don't know how to effectively fight and annul:

- Hunger;

- Climate Change;

- The Cascade of Conflicts and Migrations;

- The spread of fear in different parts of the world and the arms race already initiated by the great powers.

These four serious reasons of global unsustainability are causing insecurity, hopelessness and an intra-continental and intercontinental massive migration flow that are already putting at severe risk the existence of the democracies in the West.

As I have been saying for a long time, there are not "inaccessible mountains, insurmountable obstacles, impregnable fortresses!"

If we are not able to recreate hope and void the despair, misery and fear that plague large parts of our planet, every wall, every fortress already initiated will crumble. Nothing and no one will be able to stop the search for survival of tens and hundreds of millions of desperate people!

We, the Global Partnership for Citizenship, are the last bulwark against this terrible trend already seemingly inexorable.

If we achieve to make it germinate, grow and strengthen, we will be able to place the human being in the top vertex of the tripod of any human society (Civil Society, Market and State ("political power"), as the alpha and omega of the building of any civilization truly sustainable and with a future.

And this is the crucial point that this book highlights.

There will never be a "Global Partnership for Citizenship", our last chance against the barbarism already under way, if even civil society organizations that support and leverage it are not sustainable, viable!

And we, unfortunately, recently had a glaring example of how a civil movement that was intended to be global and humanist collapsed, which was the World Social Forum (WSF) in Porto Alegre, essential to the strengthening of democracy and of a fair and sustainable development, which aimed to be a counterweight to the Davos World Economic Forum.

The WSF collapsed due to the inability of their mentors and leaders to agree on catalyst vision, a mobilizing strategy and two or three clear and global objectives that would turn the Forum sustainable!

AMI Foundation, which I founded in 1984, is sustainable (which does not mean perennial) because it has values, principles, a vision, a strategy and clear objectives whose sole purpose is a global humanitarian action. We know what we want and, more importantly, what we do not want. Therefore, AMI may be compared to a carriage conducted by three "horses":

a) Adequate, transparent and controlled financial means;

b) A clear vision and flexibility to adapt to the new challenges and;

c) An unconquerable soul (the driver) that has and continues to stand out in giving its contribution, undoubtedly simple and modest, in order to consolidate the Global Solidarity Society, a dream of decades.

Hence, only with thousands of other sustainable civil society organizations (and with a "soul", which to me is essential to maintain sustainability), we will manage to overcome the optimism of the will to the pessimism of reason.

I believe that the authors, who I strongly congratulate, the AMI Foundation and all of those who still dare to dream and act positively, will reach together the most desired goal: a Planet and a sustainable Human Civilization, with a future...

Thank you very much.

Fernando de La Vieter Nobre, MD, PHD

Founder and President of AMI Foundation
(Global Humanitarian Action Portuguese NGO)

Professor of the Humanitarian Medicine at the
Medical School of the University of Lisbon

General Surgeon and Urologist

Conducted over 250 humanitarian missions worldwide

ACKNOWLEDGMENTS

This book is proof of how simple ideas can develop into a new paradigm with the potential to have a strong impact worldwide. Hopefully, ideas that can change the world. It is also a demonstration of how trust, passion, commitment, transparency, flexibility and cooperation can reach high standards.

It would not have been possible without the commitment and volunteering of many people. First, I have to thank Nádia for accepting my challenge. An initial introduction through Linkedin led to a 40-minute meeting in January 2013 and an immediate empathy. A strong feeling that we could be doing something memorable, at least for ourselves… One week later, we were already planning the book. Despite living only half an hour away from each other, most of the work was done remotely and after two years of hard work, we were able to finish it.

Secondly, I have to thank all the beta readers. Some were friends and others were people I have never met in person, from more than twenty countries. I would like to thank them for their interest and availability to read, proofread and, in some cases, provide valuable suggestions.

Nuno Pietra Torres, Max Daves, Isabel Saavedra, Max Mohammadi, Teresa Antunes, André Almeida, Manfred Stockmann, C. Joybell C., Ray Burch, Mario Arturo Ruiz Estrada, Artem V L, Reg Nordman, Gérard Henri Loiseau, Kenneth Meyer, Michael Stock, Tim McGettigan, Julia Myslina, Guilherme Collares Pereira, Roger Lee, Jody Turner, Maggie Boomers, Artur Reynolds Brandão, Maria João Delgado, Gbemi Akande, Vince Thompson, Mihaela Ulieru, Raquel Antunes, Paulo Manoel Lenz Cesar Protásio, Anna Gillrath-Jaeger, Joana Horta e Costa, Madalena Durão, Sofia Durão, Anna Reynolds, Cara Diemond, Mariana Vitorino, Margarida Monteiro de Barros, Carlos Bana e Costa, Francisco Lopes dos Santos, Femi Oni, Sylvia Kwan, Ana Malheiro, Chris Widner and Isabell Kiessling

It is amazing to see how the world works today. The way people get involved and spontaneously participate in projects they believe in. Probably, there are many more "missionaries" (you can understand this observation after you have read the book…) than most of us would imagine.

Therefore, I must say that I am very happy. Whatever the result of the book, this journey has already been fantastic. I have learned a lot and I have deeply enjoyed all the moments. I sincerely hope that you will like it, learn and get inspired. If so, reach out. There is a lot we can do together.

Miguel Reynolds Brandão

The Sustainable Organisation came to me in an unexpected manner, but the topic is something I had always been passionate about. The end result comes to show how powerful this information age can be and how collaboration with the sole motivation of spreading a message and create discussion can lead us to undertake two years-worth of a lot of reading, writing, debating and thinking. And it has been so inspiring!

First of all, I have to thank Miguel for having chosen me as his "partner in crime" for The Sustainable Organisation. I was thrilled to have found someone that shared a passion for creating and disseminating ideas. I also have to thank him for having been so patient with all my deadlines and travels… But, most of all, for having shown an incredible determination in achieving this goal and getting people on board.

This brings me to the beta readers. We have had incredible response and the readers were tireless in their contributions. I would like to thank them all for believing in us and for having read this book in record time. It was truly a great help. I would also like to thank Pedro Martins, Gregory Rogan and Tiago Morais for having given me their valuable contribution during the revision of the book.

I can only hope that readers enjoy this as much as I did. Throughout the whole process, we constantly had in mind that our aim is to stir thoughts, challenge the status quo and bring people together to discuss these ideas, create a debate on this paradigm and ultimately, to instil sustainability in the corporate world, but most of all, in everyone's lives.

Nádia Morais

INTRODUCTION

"No matter how insignificant the thing you have to do, do it as well as you can, give it as much of your care and attention as you would give to the thing you regard as most important. For it will be by those small things that you shall be judged." –
Mahatma Gandhi

Across the world, happiness and quality of living remain the ultimate goals of any human being, but in the current society, the rise of inequality has blocked the achievement of this goal, namely through the way that organisations are structured and developed. This rise in inequality, allied to factors like speculation, imbalanced income distribution, unfair compensation practices and lack of transparency and accountability, has led to a growing number of unhappy community members and unsustainable organisations.

This research takes on a topic deemed as crucial to all readers – from top organisational leaders to the average worker – with the aim to provide a better understanding of what causes inequality and propose ways to boost sustainability across organisations, particularly public companies listed in the stock market.

The general claim is that organisations need to adapt to the New Economy we live in to halt the trend towards unsustainability. We have been experiencing a tremendous technological evolution over the last decade, particularly in the way that people communicate. We know that communication is at the core of any organisation but we realise that organisational models have not evolved to adapt and gain leverage from this new social and technological reality. There is a clear need for a new paradigm to cope with the possibilities of a global and interconnected world.

This evolution can be done through drivers that can truly boost happiness across organisations and the communities where they operate, replacing the old drivers that characterise the Old Economy. By empowering people to look at organisations and assess them through the actual value they produce, the society as a whole can be enlightened and get involved in a movement to boost sustainability and create a new leadership model.

The Sustainable Organisation – A Paradigm for a Fairer Society revolves around three key concepts: organisations, the economy and sustainability; it focuses on how organisations can have a critical role in the definition of a wider economic model.

We hereby define organisations[1] as groups of two or more people who gather around a common purpose. These are the companies, businesses, NGOs, clubs, etc. formed for a particular purpose. Organisations are interdependent: while they have the potential to create wealth and generate a positive impact on the economy, the latter creates a conjuncture that can have a positive or negative influence in the performance of the organisation.

The economy[2], or the science of managing scarce resources, is defined as the state of a country or region in terms of the production and consumption of goods and services and the supply of money, but also as the careful management of the available resources and the activities that help determine the way scarce resources are allocated. As the state of the economy often reflects the general state of the country, this also comes as a good indicator of the health of organisations within a country.

The final concept is sustainability[3], or an organisation's capacity to last and enjoy the present without compromising the future. This has been the buzzword of the last decade and it is defined as an organisation's ability to be utilised without being completely used up or destroyed, involving methods that do not completely exhaust or extinguish natural resources; an organisation that is able to last or continue for a long time. The importance of this concept is paramount: only lasting, resourceful and renewable organisations will survive a difficult economy, much in the same way, as sustainable organisations are more likely to prosper in an enabling economy.

"True knowledge exists in knowing that you know nothing." – Socrates

WHAT INSPIRED US?

First and foremost, we have been inspired by the will to contribute towards the creation of a movement that can facilitate sustainability. In essence, we are inspired by the possibility for an individual, anywhere in the world, to be able to develop a theory and spread it across the world in just a few seconds. This is also why we have decided to publish this book as a digital tool that can trigger a communication process with the public.

DOES POWER HAVE A POSITIVE EFFECT ON HUMAN RELATIONSHIPS?

In terms of the content, we have taken inspiration from the need to fight three aspects present in this New Economy[4]. These are a deteriorating middle class, strong inequality and the high concentration of power in certain organisations. Without a high-standard competition, we believe these three elements can lead to an unstable society, job insecurity and abuse of power, respectively. In fact, we believe this concentration of power is the root of a wider issue: as concentration leads to power, power leads to corruption and injustice, which will ultimately lead to insecurity.

HOW DOES ONE DISTINGUISH POWER FROM INFLUENCE?

Considering these factors and the fact that we live at a time where technology and innovation are at the forefront of development and economic growth, it is our opinion that this changing economy has turned most organisational structures obsolete and that this has been the main contributor to the widening gap between the rich and the poor. Additionally, it is common knowledge that almost all governments are inefficient when it comes to wealth distribution and that a wider middle class is the key to economic and social sustainability.

Consequently, in a sustainable organisation where power is not concentrated in the hands of a few, people naturally become happier at work and achieve a better outcome thus producing more economic value. A strong middle class is an economic powerhouse! Therefore, with a transparent organisation of the society based on meritocracy and where the impact of each organisation can be easily measured and assessed, every citizen would be able to benefit from the same opportunities, privileges and the right to be happy.

WHO INSPIRED US?

To undertake this mission, we have taken inspiration from several philosophers, gurus, academics and CEOs who have served as an example to the corporate world. We have found it useful to take inspiration from people who have had an impact that is unrelated to organisational structures. After all, what makes a strategist become a guru is the fact that they have a transformational ability to inspire people and even, to change the way people live.

One of those examples is Mahatma Gandhi[5]. While leading India in the struggle for independence, Gandhi held a beacon to some management strategies and became more than a mere political leader: a strategist and an exemplary leader. One of the core principles we have found in Gandhi's strategy includes the creation of a vision that shared by the people by using core values like honesty and non-violence.

Gandhi identified himself with the masses, which led him to win their respect, confidence and allegiance and one of his greatest achievements was that he could easily relate to the people. These principles are closely related with the practices we advocate: living the values to create change in the current management structure and have clear goals that enable organisations to reinvent their means according to the circumstances, while encouraging all members of the organisation to believe they are key to the performance of their organisation and community – the principle of empowerment.

Nelson Mandela[6] has been another such inspirational leader, who taught many lessons to the corporate world. One of them was the core principle of always keeping our eyes on the long-term goal using flexibility to move towards that goal that we believe is worthwhile, something that we can truly see in his life path. During his 27-year incarceration, Mandela's vision of a non-racial democracy never weakened and after his release in 1990, he continued to face stiff opposition in the pursuit of his goal. Still, at every obstacle, Mandela kept his eyes set on his objective[7] and recognised that he would have to adjust his approach to the circumstances, much in the same way we believe the corporate world needs to adapt to the New Economy. Both Gandhi and Mandela are great examples of people who advocated peace as an instrument of development and the only manner to resolve the problems of humanity.

Greek philosopher Socrates[8], one of the fathers of philosophy, was another great source of inspiration. The Socratic Method was particularly inspiring. It has come into general usage as an educational strategy that involves cross-examination of students by their teacher, based on Socrates' specific pattern of seeing himself not as a teacher, but as an ignorant inquirer. On Socrates Café[9], the Socratic Method is described as a way to seek truths by our own lights, in a system that allows people to interrogate themselves from many vantage points, calling for the use of common sense and common speech to explore opinions and then offer compelling objections and alternatives, which resembles the scientific method in many ways. The reason why we find the work of Socrates such an inspiration for our own work is his concern for people. In a similar way, instead of changing people, we want to have people reach conclusions; we want to raise awareness and empower people so that they can generate their own solutions and instil change.

Furthermore, we advocate the economist Adam Smith's[10] idea that value is found "in the trouble of acquiring labour" rather than in its financial return as well as the idea that an "invisible hand"[11] guides supply and demand. As well as this, we support Robert Reich's[12] idea that organisations' most precious possessions are people, not financial assets. He believes the most important organisational element is the people working there "and what they carry around in their heads and their ability to work together".

With the exception of Reich, none of these inspirations belong to the modern world or have lived in this modern economy, but they advocate the principles and values needed to adapt to changes and attain lifelong objectives. Similarly, but deeply enrooted in the management world, we believe that Peter F. Drucker[13], considered as the father of modern management thinking, has had the foresight to prefigure the new management theories of the next fifty years. Drucker's principles of management are well alive in the current times and have been transformational to several organisations, namely setting objectives, organising, motivating and communicating, establishing measurements of performance and developing people.

Finally, we have been inspired by the brain, the very human element that defines us. The neurons, made of approximately 100 billion cells, gather and transmit electrochemical signals: motor neurons control the muscles, sensory neurons control the central nervous system and interneurons connect various neurons within the brain and spinal cord.[14] Therefore, each neuron varies in their level of influence and they are all equally important in fulfilling their mission of governing our lives. If science is so often inspired by nature in other applications, why not look at the complexity of the brain as a source of inspiration for a more balanced, efficient and sustainable organisational model?

OUR PURPOSE

We believe that, in a transparent world, a balanced distribution of the outcome produced by organisations and a stronger economic development for the whole humanity (regardless of people's location or activity) can lead to a better life. Similarly, enabling all members of the community to observe organisations and compare them with others, in an accountable and speculation-free system so that they can determine the real economic value these organisations produce, creates a transparency that will enable people to build organisations characterised by a strong and positive economic development. Balance and stability necessarily lead to more economic value.

Our ultimate goal is to empower people to look at organisations and to compare them so that organisations can be valued by what they do – free from speculation. Our hope is to enlighten people to get involved in a revolution, leading to a more sustainable model and, in turn, a fairer world. For organisations to become truly sustainable we believe it is essential to create a new organisation model: a more cooperative leader, a new way for people to cooperate inside the organisation and a new way for organisations to be measured by society.

STRUCTURE AND METHODOLOGY

"I cannot teach anybody anything; I can only make them think."
– Socrates

The book is divided in two parts. Part I provides an outlook of the current situation (the global context, the global problem and the global solutions) and Part II provides a proposal (the Sustainable Organisation Model). In Part I, we have compiled information to enable the reader to gain a deep understanding of the current situation while on Part II, we offer a model that can contribute to create and develop sustainable organisations.

In the first part, we have created an unorthodox methodology that can help readers follow our line of thought. We start by testing a series of hypotheses, making assumptions and analysing the resulting observations. Then, we outline the most important facts that support those observations and explore the myths and paradoxes that are commonly associated with these facts. Throughout the text, we raise questions to spark the reader's thought and list ideas that can be useful to surpass the problems identified throughout the chapter. In Part II, we present a model for a proposal that can help accelerate and measure the process of turning organisations sustainable.

This book has been developed in a way that enables the reader to randomly access a topic, to think about the issue and ultimately, to research it. To facilitate the process we have created an extensive table of contents. Thus, the reader can revisit relevant information and enlighten his/her curiosity. However, it is not meant to serve as a guide. Rather, it is meant to make the reader think and clarify his/her perception about the actual relevance that sustainable organisations have in the development of the society.

PART I

This part provides context on the facts that affect sustainability worldwide. Essentially, it gathers information that can instil reflection and questions.

Structurally, it lists facts, paradoxes, myths and ideas that are related with a given set of observations.

It can be read sequentially or in random.

It contains three chapters: Global Context, Global Problem and Global Solution.

Global Context: Why Change is Needed

The aim of this chapter is to present a diagnosis of the current global economic development and stability, specifically in terms of employee compensation, to provide a framework to why inequality must be tackled.

To this effect, it includes a set of observations: (1) Inequality is a Global Reality, (2) Inequality Indexes Remain Inefficient, (3) Regulation Has Failed to Have an Impact and (4) Global Efforts are Gearing Up towards Regulation.

The aim of this structure is to identify the problem under debate – rising inequality – and assess the metrics and regulation created to tackle it, with a focus on section 953(b) of the Dodd-Frank Act in

THE UNITED STATES, AS WELL AS PRESENT THE MOST RECENT MEASURES TAKEN ACROSS THE WORLD TO RESOLVE INEQUALITY.

THE MAIN OBJECTIVE IS TO RAISE THE ISSUES RELATED WITH HOW CURRENT MANAGEMENT MODELS TACKLE INEQUALITY AND IDENTIFY THE NEED BROUGHT ABOUT BY THE PRESENT ECONOMY – A TURNING POINT THAT BRINGS THE NEED TO ESTABLISH A FAIRER AND MORE TRANSPARENT DISTRIBUTION AMONG ALL MEMBERS OF THE SOCIETY.

OBSERVATION: INEQUALITY IS A GLOBAL REALITY

"Equality, rightly understood as our founding fathers understood it, leads to liberty and to the emancipation of creative differences; wrongly understood, as it has been so tragically in our time, it leads first to conformity, and then to despotism". — Barry Goldwater, former US President

"I am not an Athenian or a Greek, but a citizen of the world." — Socrates

"The problems of the world cannot possibly be solved by sceptics or cynics whose horizons are limited by the obvious realities. We need men who can dream of things that never were." — John F. Kennedy

Assessing global inequality[15], or the extent to which income and wealth are unevenly distributed among the world population, has always been challenging for researchers, mainly because different nations deal with income and wealth in different ways.

There is a rising number of sources and information available on the topic. One of them is the Luxembourg Income Study[16], which created a cross-national data archive for income and wealth. Similarly, the World Top Incomes Database[17] created by the Paris School of Economics compiles the incomes of the world's richest nations[18], while the United Nation's World Institute for Development Economics Research (UNU-WIDER[19]) was the first of the kind to tally all the major elements of household wealth at a global level. Based on data from the year 2000, the study found that the richest 1% of the world's adult population owned 39.9% of the world's household wealth.

According to a more recent study[20] by the anti-poverty charity Oxfam, the wealthiest 1% will soon own more than the rest of the world's population, as the share of the world's wealth owned by the richest 1% increased from 44% in 2009 to 48% in 2014. The organisation expects the wealthiest 1% to own more than 50% of the world's wealth by 2016, a forecast that it describes as "simply staggering" and that coincides with the start of the World Economic Forum in Davos.

FACT: THE RICHEST 1% OF THE WORLD'S ADULT POPULATION OWNED 39.9% OF THE WORLD'S HOUSEHOLD WEALTH IN 2000.

More recently, a working paper[21] by the European Central Bank verified the data on wealth distribution published in the United States and in various countries in the Eurozone based on surveys undertaken with families. Philip Vermeulen concluded that the results had been affected by the lack of responses or interviewees who tend to omit real data, but he established that the weight of the fortune owned by the top 1% and the top 5% is actually higher than what most people thought. Based on the survey, he determined that the wealthiest 1% in the United States (US) hold between 35% and 37% of the total wealth in the country, compared to the estimated 34% by previous surveys. In Europe, these figures are even higher: 33% in Germany instead of the previous 24%, 21% in Italy instead of 14% and 17% in Holland, instead of 9%.

Financial institutions have also tried to compute global wealth. The World Wealth Report[22] by Capgemini and Merril Lynch's report on Wealth Management[23], Boston Consulting Group's (BCG) Global Wealth report[24] and the Global Wealth report by the Credit Suisse Research Institute of Switzerland[25] constitute useful resources with interest findings. According to the latter, the richest 0.5% of adults hold well over a third of the world's wealth.

FACT: THE RICHEST 0.5% OF GLOBAL ADULTS HOLD OVER A THIRD OF THE WORLD'S WEALTH.

Another study, published by the Centre for Global Development, a US-based think-tank, shows that income inequality rose slightly from the late 1980s to 2005 and has been relatively flat since then, especially in terms of inequality within countries. However, this result is largely attributed to rising prosperity in China, which means the situation is far more severe. According to a report published on Forbes magazine in March 2011[26], the world's current 1,210 billionaires hold a combined wealth that equals more than half the total wealth of the 3.01 billion adults around the world. That is to say, the richest 1% hold over a third of global wealth and the world's billionaires hold a combined wealth that represents more than half of the total wealth of the world's population.

FACT: IN 2011, THE WORLD'S 1,210 BILLIONAIRES HELD A COMBINED WEALTH THAT EQUALLED MORE THAN HALF THE TOTAL WEALTH OF THE 3.01 BILLION ADULTS AROUND THE WORLD.

On top of the inequality in earnings, it has also been proven that there is an extreme level of concentration. Physicist and former researcher at a Swiss hedge fund, James B. Glattfelder[27] believes that networks are the ideal representation of complex systems and can be successfully applied to economics. His study *The Network of Global Corporate Control*[28] went viral due to the innovative use of networks to analyse shareholding relations.

He started with a database with 13 million ownership relations focusing on transnational companies and obtained a periphery which contains 75% of all the players and a centre that contains a tiny but dominant core made up of highly interconnected companies. In this core, the companies make up 95% of the total operating revenue of all the transnational companies analysed, although only 36% of the companies are present in this core.

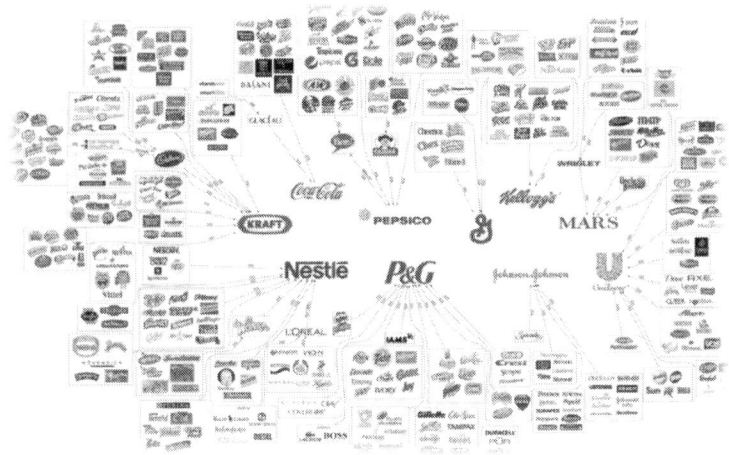

Fig. 1 The Companies that control the world[29]

Glattfelder concluded that the high degree of control is extreme and the high degree of interconnectivity of the top players in the core could pose a significant systemic risk to the global economy.

In fact, this high degree of control can be observed in different spheres. We can look at how companies control what the population of the world consumes and go as far as observe how a very restricted group of companies manages to control the world economy.

In terms of consumption, a chart published by Convergence Alimentaire (Fig. 1) shows that ten large corporations control the output of almost everything we buy. PepsiCo is a flagrant example. The corporation owns Yum Brands, which owns KFC, Taco Bell, among many others. The US$84 billion Procter & Gamble and Kraft Foods are other evident examples, while the US$200 billion food giant Nestle, owns nearly 8,000 different brands worldwide.

Looking at the economy itself, it has been argued that a very strict number of financial groups seem to dominate the world: Bank of America, JP Morgan, Citigroup, Wells Fargo, Goldman Sachs and Morgan Stanley, with a nucleus of shareholders referred to as the "big four": State Street Corporation, Vanguard Group, BlackRock and FMR (Fidelity)[30]. These "big four" control an immense number of companies, from Coca-Cola to ExxonMobil, going through companies as diverse as General Electric, McDonald's, Pfizer, Walt Disney, Verizon and Wal-Mart. The same "big four" control most European companies present in the stock exchange. On top of that, these are the very same people who seem to run large financial institutions such as the International Monetary Fund (IMF), the European Central Bank (ECB), the World Bank (WB) and even the United Nations (UN)...

There is no need to read any more to conclude that we do live in a world characterised by strong inequality and this organisational concentration of power at all levels is clearly one of the main reasons for this.

PARADOX: As the world develops and evolves – in the technological, economic and educational sense – the inequality gap becomes wider

Although global consumption has been growing at a steady pace and a global middle class is emerging in some parts of the world, the gap between the rich and the poor has still not been broken down. Also, people seem to be less and less excited with their work activities. According to a study by Deloitte's Center for Edge entitled *Unlocking the Passion of the Explorer*[31], only 11% of the US employees surveyed have the necessary attributes that lead to accelerated learning and the improvement of performance.

MYTH: Growth benefits everyone, or at least most people.

GLOBAL GAP

Although this inequality is a global reality, it is not equal across the world. While some countries have become less equal, others have become more equal. One of the tools that can be used to assess this level of inequality is the GINI index[32] (assessed later in this chapter), which is increasingly seeing its effectiveness questioned, mainly because it draws conclusions from the commonly used aggregate inequality measures, making it difficult to understand how global growth interacts with changing national and international inequality.

According to a report by *The Economist*[33], over time, the number of poor people escaping poverty is growing, but the rich are also getting richer. The report identifies different levels of growth, namely growth that helps the poorer end of revenue distribution or that hurts the poor, and growth that is equitable across the income spectrum, which can only be verified in countries like Vietnam, Nepal and the Philippines. However, the issue changes entirely when observed at a national level. Here, the question is one of growth governance – different countries manage growth in different ways, which plays a significant role in who benefits from growth and how much.

"Where globalization means, as it so often does, that the rich and powerful now have new means to further enrich and empower themselves at the cost of the poorer and weaker, we have a responsibility to protest in the name of universal freedom." – Nelson Mandela

Overall, the report identified a persistent global structure of two homogenous clusters, the poor/insecure and the prosperous/secure. It concluded that the emerging global middle class may not represent a move away from the old two-cluster, but rather a transitional phase, where some groups in richer emerging markets are shifting out of the poor/secure cluster into the secure/prosperous cluster.

On top of this, the wages of most workers are falling more and more behind those of top earners, even as average wages fail to keep pace with productivity growth, WorldWatch[34] warns. According to the organisation, these trends are highly influenced by globalisation and the economic crisis[35]. In fact, when looking at global changes cumulatively from 2000 to 2011, global real monthly average wages grew by just under a quarter, but there are considerable regional differences: wages almost doubled in Asia, increased by 18% in Africa and by 15% in Latin America and the Caribbean. Meanwhile, wages in Eastern Europe and Central Asia (including Russia) nearly tripled. In Russia, the growth that followed economic collapse only returned wages to what they had been at the beginning of the 1990s. In the Middle East, limited wage data suggest stagnation during the last decade.

FACT: IN 2000-2011, WAGES ALMOST DOUBLED IN ASIA, INCREASED BY 18% IN AFRICA AND BY 15% IN LATIN AMERICA AND THE CARIBBEAN.

Thinking about this, it is not difficult to imagine the countries with the highest hourly compensation rate. According to the US Bureau of Labor Statistics (BLS), these are found in northern and western Europe, with Norway as the one with the highest reported compensation in 2011 (US$64.15 per hour). Japan and the US are in the middle, while southern and eastern European countries, most of Asia and Latin America have a lower compensation. The Philippines has the lowest rate of the 34 countries, at US$2.01 per hour. The study also offers estimates for China (US$1.34 per hour in 2008) and India (US$1.17 per hour in 2007).

Looking at English-speaking countries, the study found that there has been a sharp increase in salaries and compensation for top corporate executives, contrary to the trend seen in other sectors. In the US alone, the top 1% of wage earners saw their annual earning go up by 156% between 1979 and 2007. For 90% of US workers, wages only advanced by 17% in the same period.

FACT: IN THE U.S., THE TOP 1% OF WAGE EARNERS SAW THEIR ANNUAL EARNINGS GO UP BY 156% BETWEEN 1979 AND 2007. FOR 90% OF U.S. WORKERS, IN CONTRAST, WAGES ADVANCED BY 17% IN THE SAME PERIOD.

Also, from 1978 to 2011, CEO compensation at the largest 350 companies in the US increased by over 725%, compared to a mere 5.7% in average worker compensation. Among the initial

12 members of the European Union, Germany was the only country where average real compensation per employee declined in 1999-2010[36].

FACT: FROM 1978 TO 2011, CEO COMPENSATION AT THE 350 LARGEST U.S. COMPANIES INCREASED MORE THAN 725%, COMPARED WITH JUST 5.7% IN AVERAGE WORKER COMPENSATION.

"The gap between wages and labour productivity and the rising inequality of wages are developments that raise fundamental questions of fairness in the economy", Michael Renner[37], a WorldWatch Senior Researcher explains. "The extremely unequal distribution of income and wealth that has emerged worldwide has profound consequences, determining who has an effective voice in matters of economics and politics and thus how countries address the fundamental challenges before them", he adds.

In the UK, for instance, the Equality Trust has been assessing the level of inequality with its annual publication, *Wealth Tracker*. In 2013, it found that the richest 1,000 people are wealthier than the poorest 40% of households, while the richest 100 have over 100 billion GBP more wealth than the poorest 30% of households. According to the Director, Duncan Exley, "wealth inequality in the UK is vast. The fact that just 100 people could have more wealth than 30% of the population is staggering. Can anything really justify just 100 people having the same wealth as almost 19 million people? Does anyone think this is a fair or efficient share of wealth?"

In the meantime, other indexes similar to GINI have been created to measure economic progress. One of the most reliable seems to be the Social Progress Index (SPI)[38]. First released in 2014, the SPI measures a comprehensive range of components of social and environmental performance and aggregates them into a framework. It incorporates four key design principles: (1) exclusively social and environmental indicators that measure social progress directly, analysing the relationship between economic development and social development; (2) outcomes not inputs; (3) holistic info that is relevant to all countries and (4) information that is actionable.

Furthermore, the index focuses on three different questions:

- Does a country provide for its people's most essential needs?
- Are the building blocks in place for individuals and communities to enhance and sustain wellbeing?
- Is there opportunity for all individuals to reach their full potential?

The findings of the research disclosed in 2015 conclude that ten countries in the world represent the "top tier" in term of social progress, with Norway, Sweden and Switzerland as the top three, which should not come as a surprise. The bottom, described as the very low social progress countries ranges from Ethiopia to the Central African Republic and represents a material step down in social progress countries, the report explains.

IDEA: Taking measures to ensure stability could assure the long-term economic growth and welfare at a global level.

American economist and Nobel Prize laureate Joseph E. Stiglitz[39], has been in the forefront of the debate on inequality. He is well known for his critical view of the management of globalisation, free-market economists and some institutions like the International Monetary Fund (IMF) and the World Bank (although he previously served as its senior vice president and chief economist). According to Stiglitz, inequalities have harmful economic effects, namely the decrease in aggregate demand, which can slow economic growth[40]. The attempt by monetary authorities to offset these effects can contribute to credit bubbles, which lead to further instability. On the other hand, reducing inequality has clear benefits, he explains. It strengthens people's sense that society is fair; it improves social cohesion and mobility and broadens support for growth initiatives.

Market dynamics, policies and developments have led to different events and evolutions, but the distance between top earners and the bottom billion continues to expand at a steady pace. In his article entitled *The Instability of Inequality*[41], Professor Nouriel Roubini sends out a warning about the dangers of this rising inequality. "Any economic model that does not properly address inequality will eventually face a crisis of legitimacy. Unless the relative economic roles of the market and the state are rebalanced, the protests of 2011 will become more severe, with social and political instability eventually harming long-term economic growth and welfare", he states.

"The great enemy of the truth is very often not the lie, deliberate, contrived and dishonest, but the myth, persistent, persuasive and unrealistic." – John F. Kennedy

IDEA: "The challenge as you get bigger is not to become so big that you become just like another one of the big carriers. Trying to stay small while getting bigger is very important. Any company that has more than 250 people in a building is in danger of starting to become impersonal. In an ideal world, 150 people are the most that should be working in one building and in one organisation, so that everyone knows each other and knows their Christian names." – Richard Branson

IDEA: Ban privileges. The rules of the game should be the same to all players, regardless of their size, location, or any other criteria.

OBSERVATION: THERE IS STILL NO EFFICIENT METRIC FOR ECONOMIC DEVELOPMENT AND/OR INEQUALITY

Different metrics have been created to measure inequality. Although they all have weaknesses that have put their efficiency into question, they remain useful in partially quantifying inequality, but also to rank countries according to their earnings, production and wealth. Under an economic perspective, they show which countries are doing better and why, to some extent.

GROSS DOMESTIC PRODUCT (GDP)

GDP has been the most widely used metric across the world. It represents the market value of all officially recognised final goods and services produced within a country in a given period and the GDP per capita is often considered as a good indicator of a country's standard of living[42]. Although it is widely used to gauge economic recession and recovery, it is not meant to measure externalities. Rather, it serves as a general metric that is not adjusted to the cost of living within a region, as it merely shows an economy's general ability to pay for externalities such as social and environmental concerns and does not account for wealth distribution, non-market transactions, the underground economy, the non-monetary economy, among other factors[43].

MYTH: A growing GDP infers economic growth.

In fact, when the former French President Nicolas Sarkozy commissioned leading economists to look into better methodologies to replace the GDP, they produced a report, entitled *Mismeasuring Our Lives: Why GDP Doesn't Add Up*[44]. The report concluded that the GDP was not doing a good job and even said that too much of a focus on this metric could send policymakers in the wrong direction.

PARADOX: The GDP measures world wealth, albeit only considering the value of final goods and services produced in a country.

Austrian Economist Frank Shostak[45] has been a fierce critic of the GDP. He believes that the metric is detached from the real world and has no value in economic analysis. "The GDP framework cannot tell us whether final goods and services that were produced during a particular period of time are a reflection of real wealth expansion or a reflection of capital consumption", he said in an article[46] published by the Ludwig Von Mises Institute. The GDP framework is an empty abstraction devoid of any link to the real world", he concluded.

FACT: THE GDP DOES NOT ACCOUNT FOR EXTERNALITIES OR SERVICES.

Much earlier, economist Simon Kuznets[47], who developed the first set of measures of national income, had already raised the failings of the GDP. In his first report to the US Congress in 1934, in a section entitled *Uses and Abuses of National Income Measurements*[48], he stated: "The valuable capacity of the human mind to simplify a complex situation in a compact characterisation becomes dangerous when not controlled in terms of definitely stated criteria". He explained at the time that quantitative measurements suggest a precision, which leads to "illusion" and "abuse". He goes on to conclude that "the welfare of a nation can therefore, scarcely be inferred from a measurement of national income". According to Kuznets, the amount of growth must be differentiated from the quality of the growth.

More recently, in an article published by the Financial Times (FT), editor David Piling[49] also criticises the use of the GDP as a metric, accusing it of having an unclear meaning. He cites economist Diane Coyle – who advocates the use of the metric as long as we grasp its limitations – as saying that "GDP is a made-up entity" and that the GDP provides that, "no sense of the trade-off between present and future", leaving us vulnerable to "tipping points". In fact, he states, one of the important things about the GDP is that is measures the flow, not the stock, without taking into account depleted resources (like the finite oil and gas resources a certain country consumed), nor does it account for externalities, like pollution. In addition, the GDP does not capture services in its calculation. Since these now account for two thirds of the output of many advanced economies, this metric can be extremely misleading, as we know it. As well as this, Coyle explains, the GDP fails to capture innovation, which is another key element in the current economic development.

According to the Head of Global Strategy at Investnet Kachary Karabell[50], Diane Coyle has described the GDP as a creation by, "all-too human economists and politicians" that shed some light on the output of nations and helped the United States and the United Kingdom fight and win the World War II by "devoting massive amounts of domestic industry to making machines of war without imperilling domestic economic life". However, Karabell believes that the largest problem with the GDP is the maximalist use of it by economists, politicians and the general public who use it as a stand-in for national success[51]. Still, he believes we are all becoming less dependent on the GDP and information about customers and their behaviour has become far more important.

Although the GDP debate has been on-going and few economists ignore its limitations, its maximisation remains as a goal in practically all economies. Piling concludes: "GDP may be anachronistic and misleading. It may fail entirely to capture the complex trade-offs between present and future, work and leisure, "good" growth and "bad" growth. (...) For the time being, we may be stuck with it".

The *Inclusive Wealth Report* 2014[52] (IWR) offers a different perspective regarding economic performance, introducing the Inclusive Wealth Index and extends beyond the GDP to help reflect sustainable development, the report explains. As well as the GDP, the Inclusive Wealth Index (IWI) factors-in measures of human and natural capital and measures human capital in levels of education, skills and abilities. Overall, the report reveals that human capital is the main source of worldwide wealth and accounts for 57% of total inclusive wealth, while natural capital – which seeks to measure the extent, health and integrity of forests, subsoil resources and other ecosystems – represents 23% of total inclusive wealth.

The latest report reveals a startling difference between the GDP and the IWI. While the first rose by 50% from 1992 to 2010, the latter only increased by a meagre 6%. This is due to small increases in human capital and "vast losses in natural capital", the report explains, stating that the adoption of this index is paramount to achieve a post-2015 sustainable development agenda.

Some examples[53] of surprising differences between the GDP and the IWI mentioned by this report include:

| Ecuador: 37% GDP vs. 17% IW |
| Guyana: 97% GDP vs. 2% IW |
| Qatar: 85% GDP vs. 53% IW |
| Tanzania: 67% GDP vs. 37% IW |
| Uganda: 95% GDP vs. 6% IW. |

Gross National Product (GNP)

The GNP is a similar metric, which allocates production based on ownership. The difference is that the GDP defines its scope according to a location, while the GNP defines its scope according to ownership. However, in a global context, they are equivalent terms.

According to Karabell, Robert Kennedy[54] himself had made a passionate plea to stop using GNP as an absolute measure of national greatness. He said that, although it performs its task as a metric of how much stuff a country makes, "it does not allow for the health of our children, the quality of their education, or the joy of their play… It measures everything except that which makes life worthwhile".

Gini Coefficient

The GINI coefficient/ratio has been a popular metric in that it considers factors ignored by the metrics aforementioned. It consists on a measurement of statistical dispersion, which measures inequality among values of a frequency distribution (for instance, the levels of income). A GINI coefficient of zero expresses perfect equality, where all values are the same (i.e. everyone has the same income) while a GINI coefficient of one (100%) expresses maximal inequality among values (i.e. one person has all the income).

For OECD countries in the late 2000s, the income GINI coefficient ranged between 0.24 and 0.49, with Slovenia and Chile as the highest. African countries had the highest pre-tax GINI coefficients in 2008-2009, with South Africa as the world's highest at 0.7. The global income inequality GINI coefficient in 2005 has been estimated to be between 0.61 and 0.68 by various sources.

FACT: IN 2008-2009, SOUTH AFRICA HAD THE WORLD'S HIGHEST GINI COEFFICIENT

In the US, in the late 2000s, the fourth highest measure of income inequality was registered, out of the 34 OECD countries. According to the Census Bureau[55], the GINI index ranged from 0.21 to 0.65 across the US in 2010. According to UNICEF, Latin America and the Caribbean region had the highest net income GINI index in the world at 48.3. The remaining regional averages were sub-Saharan Africa (44.2), Asia (40.4), Middle East and North Africa (39.2), Eastern Europe and Central Asia (35.4) and High-income countries (30.9)[56].

However, many issues also arise when interpreting a GINI coefficient. The same value may result from many different distribution sources, which means the demographic structure should also be taken into account when assessing the coefficient. Countries with an ageing population or a baby boom, experience an increasing pre-tax GINI coefficient even if real income distribution for working adults remains constant.

FACT: WHEN USING THE GINI COEFFICIENT, THE SAME VALUE MAY

RESULT FROM DIFFERENT DISTRIBUTION SOURCES.

Nevertheless, this coefficient is widely used in fields like sociology, economics, health science, ecology and engineering. For example, the education GINI index estimates inequality in education for a given population to discern trends in social development through educational attainment over time. From a study of 85 countries, Mali had the highest education GINI index of 0.92 in 1990 (very high inequality in education levels), while the US had the lowest education inequality index of 0.14. Between 1960 and 1990, South Korea, China and India had the fastest drop in terms of the education inequality GINI index.

PARADOX: Assessments based on the GINI coefficient result in the conclusion that some countries with a traditionally low average quality of life are showing more equality among their population.

At the 2011 World Economic Forum in Davos, the Conference Board highlighted income inequality as one of the most serious challenges worldwide[57]. It analysed world income inequality using three methods. Firstly, they calculated the income gap between rich and poor countries, reaching a difference named "the income gap", which can be tracked over time. Secondly, they calculated the overall world income inequality using the GINI coefficient and finally, they calculated income inequality in each country and compared all the countries. However, they concluded that, because it is possible that income inequality within a country increases at the same time as the gap between the average income of that country and the average income in richer country shrink, researchers need to look at income inequality in each country individually before they compare results between countries.

Similar in concept, the GINI coefficient of opportunity measures inequality of opportunity[58]. In 2003, it was reported that Italy and Spain exhibited the largest opportunity inequality GINI index among advanced economies. Another GINI measure is income mobility[59], to estimate whether the income inequality GINI coefficient is temporary or permanent and to what extent a country or region enables economic mobility to its people so that they can move from one income quartile to another over time. This is called the Shorrocks index[60]. A 2010 study using social security income data for the US and GINI-based Shorrocks indexes concludes that its income mobility has had a complicated history, primarily due to mass influx of women into the country's labour force after World War II.

FACT: THE GINI COEFFICIENT MEASURES NET INCOME, NOT NET WORTH, SO MOST OF A NATION'S WEALTH CAN STILL BE CONCENTRATED IN THE HANDS OF A FEW.

The problem is that, even in rich countries, the GINI coefficient measures net income, not net worth, so the majority of a nation's wealth can still be concentrated in the hands of a small number of people, even if income distribution is relatively equal. Nevertheless, the coefficient can be useful to help track poverty levels. In addition, it can be compared to the GDP: if the GDP increases, it could imply that people in a country are doing better. However, if the GINI coefficient is also rising, it suggests that the majority of the population may not be experiencing an increased income.

FACT: THE GINI INDEX CANNOT BE USED TO EFFICIENTLY MEASURE INEQUALITY WITHIN NATIONS WITHOUT A PREVIOUS ASSESSMENT OF THEIR INDIVIDUAL CONTEXT.

GROSS NATIONAL HAPPINESS (GNH)
Gross National Happiness (GNH)[61] is another interesting metric. It was designed in an attempt to define an indicator and concept that could measure quality of life or social progress in more

holistic and psychological terms than the GDP, which simply values all officially recognised goods and services produced within a country in a given period. GNH stands out because it measures wellbeing and happiness, motivated by the notion that these concepts are more relevant than objective measures like consumption.

FACT: THE GNH ATTEMPTS TO MEASURE QUALITY OF LIFE AND SOCIAL PROGRESS BASED ON WELLBEING AND HAPPINESS.

The term was coined in 1972 by Bhutan's fourth Dragon King, who opened the country to the age of modernisation. It was used in the country until 2013, when it was abandoned in favour of more standard development initiatives. When in force, proposed policies in the country had to pass a GNH review based on a GNH impact statement. The Bhutanese grounding in Buddhist ideals suggests that the beneficial development of human society takes place when material and spiritual development occurs side by side to complement and reinforce each other.

The four pillars of GNH are the promotion of sustainable development preservation and the promotion of cultural values, conservation of the natural environment and establishment of good governance. Through collaboration with an international group of scholars and empirical researchers, the Centre for Bhutan Studies[62] further defined these four pillars with greater specificity into eight general contributors to happiness— physical, mental and spiritual health; time-balance, social and community vitality, cultural vitality, education, living standards, good governance and ecological vitality.

Moreover, the concept is transcultural – a nation does not need to be Buddhist to value sustainable development, cultural integrity and ecosystem conservation. Although the GNH framework reflects its Buddhist origins, it is solidly based upon the empirical research literature of happiness, positive psychology and well-being.

A second-generation GNH concept, treating happiness as a socio-economic development metric, was proposed in 2006 by

Med Jones[63], the President of International Institute of Management. The metric measures socioeconomic development by tracking seven development areas including the nation's mental and emotional health. GNH value is proposed to be an index function of the total average per capita of the following measures: economic wellness, environmental wellness, physical wellness, mental wellness, workplace wellness, social wellness and political wellness. According to the FT's piling, the GNH looks like an attempt to cover up Bhutan's poor performance, and comes well below the Human Development Index[64], which takes into account factors like life expectancy, literacy, education and standards of living – and puts Bhutan in 104th in the world.

MEDIAN VERSUS MEAN

The use of averages to express an amount that is typical for a group of people or things has been widely considered as a good indicator, as it summarises a large amount of data into a single value and indicates that there is some variability around this value. However, this mathematical tool, the mean, also becomes an inappropriate measurement of the average when there is a great deal of variability of a set of data. Here, the median becomes a useful alternative, as it refers to the midpoint in a set of values arranged in order of magnitude.

FACT: THE MEAN IS NO LONGER USEFUL WHEN THERE IS A GREAT DEAL OF VARIABILITY IN A SET OF DATA.

Nevertheless, we still rely too much on averages nowadays, although they tell us practically nothing specific and are likely to give us a misleading big picture. When calculating compensations, namely the CEO-to-worker compensation ratio, the values in the data set are usually spread out. Therefore, the result will not necessarily be revealing.

However, Payscale[65] believes that the best practice is to first consider the median – the so-called midpoint – because the mean or average can be too sensitive to outliers, while the median would be less affected by them. In its turn, the

Economic Policy Institute (EPS) states that, although it is not possible to measure the actual wages and benefits of any particular firm's workforce (although we see this as a myth), the best practice would be to use a measure of annual compensation to obtain a successful sample, where the average hourly earnings of workers are observed and then converted into a full-time, full-year wage plus benefits – the measure of annual compensation.

EPI[66] used data from the Bureau of Economic Analysis (BEA) and the Bureau of Labor Statistics (BLS) to create their own proxy and an industry-specific compensation-to-wage ratio, by dividing total compensation by total wage and salary in each industry. To obtain the average CEO compensation, the EPI used executive compensation data from the ExecuComp database from Compusat[67], a division of Standard & Poor's, which contains data on compensation for the top five executives at public companies in the US that are part of the S&P 1500 Index. To calculate the ratio, EPI divided the CEOs' compensation by the annual compensation for the typical worker within an industry.

PALMA RATIO

In an article published by the *Ethics & International Affairs* (EIA) journal[68], Stiglitz outlines a proposal, together with Michael W. Doyle, the Director of the Columbia Global Policy Initiative and the Harold Brown Professor of International Affairs, Law and Political Science at Columbia University[69]. They propose a new goal – Goal Nine – that could be integrated in the Millennium Goals: to eliminate extreme inequality at the national level in every country.

For this goal to take effect, they propose two specific targets. First, they propose the reduction of extreme income inequalities in all countries by 2030 such that, the post-tax income of the top 10% is no more than the post-transfer income of the bottom 40%. Secondly, they propose the establishment of a public commission in every country by 2020 that will assess and report on the effects of national inequalities, creating a national dialogue on what should be done to address the inequalities that are most relevant to the particular country.

According to the authors, the best indicator for this would be the Palma Ratio[70]. The Palma ratio is defined as the ratio of the richest 10% of the population's share of gross national income divided by the poorest 40%'s share, thus focusing on the extremes of inequality – the ratio of incomes at the very top to those at the bottom. It is based on the work of the Chilean economist Gabriel Palma, who found that middle class incomes almost always represent about half of gross national income, while the other half is split between the richest 10% and poorest 40%, although the share of the two groups varies across countries. However, across continents, a Palma ratio of one is an ideal reached in only a few countries.

Hence, the Palma ratio addresses the GINI index's over-sensitivity to changes in the middle of the distribution and insensitivity to changes at the top and bottom, and thus provides a more accurate reflection of the impact of income inequality on society as a whole.

OTHER METRICS

In 1989, Herman Daly and John B. Cobb developed the Index of Sustainable Economic Welfare (ISEW)[71], which takes into account various other factors such as the consumption of non-renewable resources and the degradation of the environment. Something similar has been applied in Singapore, where President Tony Tan proposed, in 2013, that in addition to building up substantial financial reserves, Singapore would focus on building up its social reserves.

Other indicators[72] of emotion analogue to economic progress have also been supported by a number of NGOs like the UK's New Economics Foundation[73]. The Gallup Poll[74] system also collects data on well-being on a national and international scale, while the Genuine Progress Indicator (GPI)[75] has been suggested to replace or supplement the GDP as a measure of economic growth. It is designed to take fuller account of the health of a nation's economy by incorporating environmental and social factors, which are not measured by GDP. For instance, some models of GPI decrease in value when the poverty rate increases[76].

The GPI is an attempt to measure whether the environmental impact of the products produced and consumed in a country is a negative or positive factor in economic health, and also account for the people currently dependent on the government for support. Businesses are beginning to expand services/products that have actually resulted in the improvement of the environment and are starting to take ecological transparency seriously enough to embed it in their strategic thinking. GPI advocates claim that it can more reliably measure economic progress, as it distinguishes between the overall "shifts in the 'value basis' of a product, adding its ecological impacts into the equation."

The United Nations (UN) have also contributed to the creation of different metrics with the Human Development Index (HDI)[77]. It is a way of measuring development by combining indicators of life expectancy, educational attainment and income into a composite index. What makes this index unique is the fact that it is a single statistic, which has to serve as a frame of reference for both social and economic development. It sets a minimum and a maximum for each dimension – the goalposts – and then shows where each country stands in relation to these goalposts, expressed as a value between zero and one.

Finally, the Better Life Index[78], developed by the Organisation for Economic Cooperation and Development (OECD) allows users to compare the performance of countries according to 11 criteria ranging from income and housing to health and work-life balance.

The list of measurements created to assess wealth and inequality, is exhaustive and these are only the most discussed examples. What seems obvious is that, while on the one hand, there is a continuous effort and interest in evaluating the wealth of a country and the level of inequality resulting from that wealth, none of these creations has been able to do in an efficient manner.

In Coyle's words, a new way to reflect economic reality should be invented, using the "dashboard approach", where voters decide what is important and politicians then craft policies to achieve the desired results.

IDEA: Indexes have not proved successful when comparing different realities; specific accounts must be created to take into account the specificities of each country, measuring welfare and happiness as not depending solely from financial wealth.

(Your comments ideas, suggestions and participation are welcome at http//www.thesustainableorganisation.com)

OBSERVATION: REGULATION HAS FAILED TO HAVE AN IMPACT

"You know, it's just too complicated. We don't really have the quantitative tools to do that." – Ben Bernanke, Chairman of the US Federal Reserve, talking about the calculation of the CEO-to-worker ratio proposed by the SEC.

Following the definite assertion that we live in a world characterised by strong inequality, governments and entities have attempted to regulate the corporate world to expose this rising inequality. These measures include the disclosure of salaries, already used in the United Kingdom, United States, Germany and Canada, but also the "say on pay" vote[79][80], used to approve CEO pay packages. Additionally, the "bonus malus" system[81], whereby executives carry downside risk as well as potential upside rewards has been proposed, as well as progressive taxation, the concept of maximum wage and debt like compensation. Finally, the indexation of operating performance, to make bonus targets business cycle independent and the setting of compensation by independent committees have also been discussed.

THE NEED FOR REGULATION

The issue of executive compensation started being widely criticised in the US around 2005. By 2007, a study by the University of Florida had found that highly paid CEOs improve company profitability as opposed to executives making less for similar jobs. However, a study by Andersoon and Batemann published in the *Journal of Organisational Behaviour* found that highly paid executives are more likely to behave cynically and show tendencies of unethical performance. In addition, in 2010, a joint study by Northeastern University[82] found that employee productivity decreases as the disparity between CEO and worker pay increases, creating the perception that all the value for the organisation is being created by the CEO.

It seems unanimous that something needs to be done to tackle this issue. This also becomes more important in bad times, when workers feel the impact of the recession – wages in the US have been flat for years, while CEO pay has risen substantially. In addition, the explosion in executive pay definitely does not seem to be justified by stock market results or company performance.

In the meantime, a new study published by the *Harvard Business Review* found that while American CEOs make nearly 350 times as much as regular workers, most Americans think they make 30 times as much. The study used data from 40 countries and looked at perceived pay gaps across 16 countries and compared them to the actual pay gap. While the gap in the United States, between perceived pay and actual pay, is the largest, other countries also perceive quite large pay gaps[83][84]. According to the study, the ideal ratio would mean that CEOs should only make seven times the amount of money average workers make. Switzerland has the second-largest pay gap between top executives and average workers, and Germany comes third.

The study, by Chulanlongkorn University's Sorapop Kiatpongsan and Harvard Business School's Michael Norton, brings more unexpected evidence regarding "what size gaps people desire" when it comes to pay. In Australia, respondents would like to see a ratio of 8.3 times, although the ratio across the countries is nearly half at 4.6 times. In addition, the desired ratio is more than 400% higher the one registered in egalitarian Nordic countries such as Denmark.

FACT: THE RISE IN EXECUTIVE PAY DOES NOT GO HAND IN HAND WITH RISING STOCK MARKET RESULTS OR COMPANY PERFORMANCE.

Overall, the impact of this high disparity has already been analysed: it was found that wide gaps in compensation could affect employee morale, productivity and turnover. It is also expected to encourage boards to consider the relationship between CEO pay and that of the average employee. Companies with high pay ratios will have to explain and justify their ratio to their shareholders. In an article published by Market Place it was reported that some business leadership experts, including Bill George, the former CEO of the medical device giant Medtronic, said that wide pay gaps can erode trust inside companies and hobble their performance. However, George is not a fan of ratios; instead, he urges boards of directors to assure that CEO pay is aligned with the company's performance

FACT: WIDE GAPS IN COMPENSATION AFFECT EMPLOYEE MORALE.

As well as company size, there are numerous factors to consider that influence CEO-to-employee ratios. These include industry sector, job mix and geographic location. In their current form, the rules defining how the CEO-to-employee pay ratio is calculated have the potential to favour companies with factors that create lower ratios. For example, the ratio will benefit companies in geographic locations with higher labour costs, and those in industries with higher-paying jobs, as well as companies that outsource low-paying jobs. As with any government-mandated financial reporting requirement, the ratio has the potential to be manipulated, miscalculated and misinterpreted.

According to a report by the Hay Group on executive compensation[85], on the whole, the pay multiple seems to reflect variations in average employee pay, rather than CEO pay, which in turn reflects the relationship between the complexity of products or services offered by a company and how close to mass consumers the company is. Moreover, the report found that there is no consistent correlation between pay equality and performance, even within a sector, which suggests that a 'one size fits all' CEO pay as a multiple of employee pay approach "simply will not work or be helpful". It also suggests that blanket explanations as to how CEO salary levels are set needed to be examined more closely.

THE POLEMIC DODD-FRANK ACT

All the talk about the CEO-to-worker pay rate was brought to light by the Dodd-Frank investor protection and financial industry reform legislation. He addressed the issue of CEO compensation by requiring shareholders to vote to approve executive compensation and golden parachute compensation, and requiring companies to disclose the pay-for-performance ratio and the ratio between the CEO's total compensation and the total compensation for all company workers.

The most polemic measure has been Section 953(b) of the Dodd-Frank Wall Street Reform and Consumer Protection Act, which has been under the limelight due to the sheer controversy it has caused within the Securities and Exchange Commission (SEC). According to this Act, companies will have to file reports with the SEC to disclose the annual total compensation of the CEO, the median annual total compensation for all employees (except the CEO) and a ratio of these two metrics – the CEO-to-worker ratio[86]. The provision passed with the aim of exposing the disparity in income within public companies and to help investors evaluate these companies better. However, the SEC has yet to issue the proposed rules, despite the initial deadline being July 2012[87].

The mandate that companies will have to disclose the CEO-to-worker pay ratio was the factor that made the rule stay at a standstill since it was first discussed in the SEC. This was before it finally moved along to its final stages in September 2013, when SEC commissioners voted to propose the rule, although "each company would have the flexibility to determine the median annual total compensation of its employees in a way that best suits its particular circumstances".

AFL-CIO[88], the umbrella federation of US unions, is calling for regulators to implement the rule and already published a White Paper[89], a report to inform about an issue and presenting the entity's philosophy on the matter, backing the proposal. According to the document, there are several investor-related risks associated with high levels of CEO compensation, namely additional financial expenses that will come out of the shareholders' pockets and incentives for unnecessary risks. The paper maintains that making the disclosure of the pay ratios mandatory provides many material benefits to investors and shareholders, as well as a good indicator of company performance and a clearer picture of compensation and responsible employment practices. Additionally, transparency would encourage companies to moderate the level of CEO pay and compensate the executives according to their performance.

FACT: TRANSPARENCY FACILITATES MODERATION AND COULD HELP COMPENSATE EXECUTIVES ACCORDING TO THEIR PERFORMANCE.

The president of the organisation, Richard Trumka[90], said: "Astronomical CEO pay is based on the false idea that the success of a corporation is due to one CEO genius. In reality, all employees create value, and CEO pay levels should be more in line with the rest of their company's employee pay structure. CEOs should be paid as a member of the team, not a superstar"[91]. In fact, this measure is not new: in the 1980s, management guru Peter Drucker had advocated capping the ratio of CEO pay to average worker pay at 20 to 1. According to the Drucker Institute, beyond this figure, resentment kicks in[92].

HARSH CRITICISM

"While the Dodd-Frank bill improved matters, it went nowhere far enough: the problems continue, and as long as they continue, our economy is at risk".
Joseph E. Stiglitz

Despite the obvious reality, the Dodd-Frank Act was received by a group of disgruntled shareholders who took little time to start voicing their opinion on excessive CEO pay, especially in the US and the UK, in what is already being called a "shareholder Spring". Shareholders at Citigroup voted to reject their CEO Vikram Pandit's pay package, saying he was collecting millions while the company floundered[93].

PARADOX: "Unfortunately, it is not possible to measure the actual wages and benefits of any particular firm's US workforce, let alone the wages and benefits of its worldwide workforce, in order to compute the ratio of CEO compensation to worker compensation in a particular firm"...

Companies are saying that they have a rough sense of their internal pay ratios, but they argue that their global workforces and varied payroll systems make calculating the median cumbersome, if not virtually impossible. What's more, they say, disclosing pay ratios would make them easy targets for CEO pay critics. Some opponents go on to say that, the measure could be used as a political tool to attack companies, while companies say that calculating this ratio will be expensive and slow.

However, companies whose boards already restrain the ratio between the CEO's salary and that of the average worker maintain that the task is not that complex. "It doesn't take months and months and millions of dollars to calculate this. It's a relatively straightforward process that takes a few days", said Mark Ehrnstein, a VP at Whole Foods Market Inc., which instituted an executive salary cap ten years ago. The company keeps a database that tracks each worker's salary and bonus to ensure that no employee makes more than 19 times the average. That means the typical full-time worker earned about US$38,000 last year and no one earned more than US$721,000. Nevertheless, the cap does not factor in stock options or pension benefits, which would be required under the proposed rule, and it considers average, rather than median salaries.

"It doesn't take months and millions of dollars to calculate this [CEO-to-worker ratio]. It's a relatively straightforward process that takes a few days". Mark Ehrnstein, VP at Whole Foods Market Inc.

"It's embarrassing that they pay their CEO 500 times what they pay their typical worker, especially if the company's performance has been mediocre", said New Jersey Senator Robert Menendez, the author of the provision. In fact, total direct compensation for 248 CEOs at public companies rose 2.8% last year, to a median of US$10.3 million, according to an analysis by the WSJ and Hay Group. A separate AFL-CIO analysis of CEO pay across a broad sample of S&P 500 firms showed the average CEO earned 380 times more than the typical US worker. In 1980, the figure was 42.

"It's embarrassing that they pay their CEO 500 times what they pay their typical worker, especially if the company's performance has been mediocre", New Jersey Senator Robert Menendez.

An article on CSWire Talkback[94] states that Rep. Nan Hayworth, the former US Representative for New York's 19th congressional district, had introduced a bill to repeal this disclosure rule before the SEC can write the necessary regulations to enforce it. The bill has already passed a key house subcommittee.

Meanwhile, corporate lobbyists have been complaining that the reporting requirement will be overly costly to fulfil and will provide no real benefits to investors. It is hard to buy the argument about cost, some argue, as companies are required to collect and maintain their employees' compensation data for accounting and tax purposes.

In their turn, advocates of high executive compensation say that, the global war for talent and the rise of private equity firms can explain much of the increase in executive pay. For example, while in conservative Japan, a senior executive has few alternatives to his current employer, in the US, it is acceptable and even admirable for a senior executive to jump between competitors, to a private equity firm or a private equity portfolio company. Portfolio company executives take a pay cut but are routinely granted stock options for ownership of 10% of the portfolio company, contingent on a successful tenure. Rather than signalling a conspiracy, defenders argue that the increase in executive pay is a mere by-product of supply and demand for executive talent. However, US executives make substantially more than their European and Asian counterparts.

Four years after Dodd-Frank became law, in July 2014, companies were still not putting the CEO-to-worker ratio into effect. The delay prompted 13 US senators to write to the SEC in November, urging it to approve a rule to implement the law, saying that incomes for the top 1% of earners have gone up by over 86% over the last 20 years, while incomes for the other 99% have grown by less than 7%. "Investors need to know to what extent skyrocketing disparities between CEO and worker pay are justified", they said.

Meanwhile, the law is being accused of having turning the US economy even more fragile, specifically in terms of the planned protection to "too big to fail" companies.

US' WHOPPING FIGURES

According to the Economic Policy Institute (EPI), CEOs at the United States' 350 biggest companies were paid 231 times more than the average private sector worker in 2011. AFL-CIO's Executive Pay Watch report went further to say that the ratio between CEOs of the S&P 500 Index and US workers, widened to 380 times in 2011 from 343 in 2010. Another report by Bloomberg states that the pay gap went up from 20 to one in the 1950s to 42 to 1 in 1980, to a whopping 120 to 1 in 2000.

FACT: CEOS AT THE US' 350 BIGGEST COMPANIES WERE PAID 231 TIMES MORE THAN THE AVERAGE PRIVATE SECTOR WORKER IN 2011.

The idea that the situation is bound to get worse comes from a look at its evolution. If we think that, in 1980, the average large company CEO only received 42 times the average worker's pay and look at the economic situation then and now, and the astronomical figures observed at the current time, the future does not look very bright. In fact, the gap between the CEOs and average workers has continued to expand. In 2011 alone, American CEOs saw their overall compensation increase in the midst of a hard financial crisis. If we look back a few more decades, the reality is even more shocking. CEO pay jumped by more than 725% between 1978 and 2011, compared to a 5.7% growth in worker compensation that period!

FACT: BETWEEN 1978 AND 2011, CEO PAY WENT UP BY MORE THAN 725%!

The EPI used a measure of CEO compensation that includes the values of stock options granted to an executive, and reported the CEO-to-worker ratio was 18.3-to-1 in 1965, before peaking at 411.3 to 1 in 2000 and settling at 209 to 1 in 2011. As demonstrated by another analysis from the EPI, hourly wage and compensation for lower-level employees remained stagnant until 2009, even as worker productivity has risen sharply. The report states further that in 2011, workers' pay saw an increase of just 2.8% in 2011. In fact, in 2010, the richest 1% captured 93% of the nation's income gains.

The Bank of South Carolina discloses a median salary at the company of just under US$52,000 a year[95]. The bank pays its CEO less than a quarter million dollars a year, not so much in the grand scheme of banking, with a low ratio of less than 5 to 1. In a recent government filing, Northwestern Corporation, a utility in Montana, said it pays its CEO 19 times the typical employees' salary. Rough estimates of some other companies put executive pay ratios dramatically higher, with some 300 to 1 and beyond. The companies that might have alarmingly large ratios are not rushing to do the calculations, at least not until the government forces them to do so.

THE FUTURE OF THE DODD-FRANK ACT

Companies under the limelight are worried that these ratios will be ranked in ascending order and splashed across websites and other media. If this happens, the companies with the highest ratios could well face public scorn. Meanwhile, by law, the SEC is supposed to come up with a system to calculate the ratio, especially as most companies are not willing to do the math.

FACT: COMPANIES WITH HIGHER RATIOS ARE MORE PRONE TO PUBLIC SCORN.

What remains certain is that corporate America has been resisting the mandate proposed by the Act, under the justification that it would be a logistical nightmare, too complex and utterly meaningless, although the public calls this "a ridiculous excuse". However, earlier in October 2013, the SEC proposed a strong, common sense rule that tells the companies to follow the law. The proposal addresses concerns about complexity by giving corporations clear guidance and sufficient flexibility to compute the ratio without undermining the law's intent – giving the public a clear picture of the gaps between pay at the top and at the median.

The difficulty around the presentation of the median workers' pay comes as this was the very fact that postponed the approval of the regulation. According to the top public companies wanting to push back the rule, it would be extremely difficult to calculate the median worker's pay. According to the Bloomberg columnist Matt Levine, this is "an absurd objection". "You are a public company. You have professional accountants. You probably keep track of how much you pay people", he says. "How hard can it possibly be to compute a median? Excel actually has a function that will do that", he stated.

There is no doubt this rule could bring a lot of useful information, but it is undeniable that most of it is already known, especially within the companies. The hope is that this will raise some sort of self-awareness to CEOs themselves and shareholders, leading to a fairer compensation that is linked to the company's performance and that can be spread across the company more evenly.

It has become publicly known that the ratio is far from being fair. Across the S&P 500 Index of companies, the average multiple of CEO compensation that of rank-and-file workers, is 204, up by 20% since 2009, according to data compiled by Bloomberg. CEOs at eight companies were paid more than 1,000 times the average worker pay in their industries. These were J.C. Penney, Abercrombie & Fitch, Simon Property Group, Oracle, Starbucks, CBS Corp., Ralph Lauren Corp. and Nike Inc.

The bigger issue here is that this disparity does not seem to reflect the CEOs value relative to their companies. While the pay ratio of the 250 largest companies in the S&P 500 index ranges from 1,795:1 (J.C. Penney's Ron Johnson) to 173:1

(Agilent Technologies' William Sullivan), Agilent shares have risen 49% over 2012, while J.C. Penney's have fallen 73%.

It thus comes as no surprise that all across Wall Street, groups have gathered to fight the Dodd-Frank provision. The most obvious reason for this seems to be that they want to avoid providing information for the larger community – society, in fact – thus strengthening the argument that the lion's share of corporate profits goes to top management.

Management guru Peter Drucker, advised companies to stick to a ratio of 20:1 between the pay of the CEO and that of the average worker. That is "the limit beyond which they cannot go if they don't want resentment and failing morale to hit their companies", he wrote. Although his standard was in line with the ratios of the 1970s and early 1980s, today it seems minor: in 2012 the ratio was about 350:1, down from where it was before the 2008 recession.

Although the ridiculous salaries may not be any news, it is expected that the SEC's mandate will serve a social purpose. According to Meredith Cross, a corporate lawyer who has worked at the SEC, "requiring companies to post potentially embarrassing information … can be a very powerful motivator to change corporate behaviour… There is a significant risk that people will keep pushing for it".

Providing this information would allow investors to more accurately judge the effect of pay structures on company performance, and would inform investors' votes on executive pay – it would become a benchmark for determining whether executive pay is excessive. Moreover, it would help regulators and policy makers detect bubbles and crashes, as these often correlate to widening pay gaps.

In November 2013, after years of delays, the SEC voted to enact the polemic provision of the Dodd-Frank Act on CEO compensation, finally requiring corporations to disclose the amount their CEOs make compared to the salary of the median worker. The response following the announcement was no surprise either: the US Chamber of Commerce and other big business organisations are afraid and fighting back, while investors rub their hands at the prospect of getting valuable information that can help them determine which companies overload at the top.

The most recent developments on the implementation of the Act include the Government's Accountability Office (GAO) call out for the Federal Reserve Bank and other regulators to finalise the key provisions of the Act that are designed to decrease government support to big banks and improve oversight. The study is the first of two that the agency is conducting to address concerns about "too big to fail". The report notes that, "effectiveness remains uncertain", while so many other provisions (…) remain incomplete".

FACT: THE EFFECTIVENESS AND COMPLETENESS OF DODD-FRANK REMAINS UNCERTAIN.

In the meantime, CEOs in the United States continue to break records, with the results from a leading annual survey on executive pay stating that, for the first time ever, the 10 highest-paid CEOs in the US received over US$100 million in compensation last year and two took home billion-dollar pay checks. The highest-paid boss in 2012 was Mark Zuckerberg, the founder of Facebook, with over US$2.27 billion, more than US$6 million a day.

A poll on pay and other forms of compensation for 2,259 US CEOs undertaken by GMI, found an average rise of 8.47% less than the double-digit growth they have enjoyed for the past two years, but this hides a complex picture: this year's top-earners far outstripped the ones below them by making fortunes on share options as the stock markets bounced back. The report states: "While stock options are intended to align the interests of senior executives with shareholders, the unintended consequence of these grants is often windfall profits that come from small share-price increases," GMI said in its report.

PARADOX: The increase in executive pay is a mere by-product of supply and demand for executive talent...

IDEA: The disclosure of the CEO-to-worker ratio is expected to create pressure in the industry to reward companies with more reasonable salary hierarchies, putting overpaid executives in the spotlight. It could actually be a game-changer for out-of-control inequality.

(Comment our ideas, give suggestions and participate, at
http//www.thesustainableorganisation.com)

OBSERVATION: GLOBAL EFFORTS ARE GEARING UP TOWARDS REGULATION

"Laws too gentle are seldom obeyed; too severe, seldom executed." –Benjamin Franklin

Several nations across the world have been trying to tackle inequality, namely the widening gap between the fortunes earned by CEOs when compared to the average compensation paid to company workers. Market dynamics, policies and development have all led to different events and evolutions, but the distance between top-earners and the bottom billion has continued to expand at a steady pace across the globe.

FACT: THE DISTANCE BETWEEN TOP-EARNERS AND THE BOTTOM BILLION CONTINUES TO EXPAND AT A STEADY PACE.

NORTH AMERICA

As mentioned in the previous section of this chapter, the United States (US) is where the issue of the inequality in compensation has been discussed the most, especially regarding the Dodd-Frank provision. Across the country, the CEO-to-worker ratio is estimated to be at 231 to 1, which means CEOs at America's 350 biggest companies were paid 231 times as much as the average private sector employee in 2011, earning an average of US$12.9 million in total over the year. Compared to 2010, average CEO pay rose by 14%.

According to the US Bureau for Labour Statistics wage data, typical worker pay was US$34,053 for all occupations in 2011. The US Social Security Administration estimates the national average wage index for 2011 at 42,979.61, 3.13% higher than the index for 2010. The estimated GINI index for the US was 0.47 and, for the late 2000s – the US had the fourth-highest measure of income inequality, out of the 34 OECD countries measured. In terms of its GDP, it was calculated at approximately US$15 trillion[96].

In Canada, the top 100 CEOs were paid 27% more in 2010 than in 2009, which has given rise to a great deal of controversy in the country. A report was published by the Canadian Centre for Policy Alternatives, but no measures have been taken so far.

The estimated CEO-to-worker pay ratio is at 189:1, which means that the highest paid CEOs in Canada are now making nearly 200 times the average Canadian wage. The 100 highest paid CEOs whose companies are listed on the S&P/TSX composite index made an average of US$8.38 million in 2010, according to the Canadian Centre for Policy Alternatives. It's also a 27% raise from the US$6.6 million average compensation for the top 100 CEOs in 2009.

According to the report by the Canadian Centre for Policy Alternatives, an average Canadian made US$44,366 in 2010 working full time. The country's GINI index was estimated to be 0.32, while GDP is estimated to be at around US$1.73 trillion.

FACT: CEOS AT AMERICA'S 350 BIGGEST COMPANIES WERE PAID 231 TIMES AS MUCH AS THE AVERAGE PRIVATE SECTOR EMPLOYEE IN 2011.

AUSTRALASIA
In Australia, shareholders can vote against the pay rises of board members, but the vote is non-binding; also, the shareholders can sack some or all of the board members. The Australian Council of Trade Unions (ACTU) published a study where it observed "an extraordinary rise in executive salaries in Australia over the past 10 years with a widening gap between what CEOs personally earn and what they choose to pay their employees". The report states that the average total remuneration of a CEO of a top 50 company listed on the Australian Securities

Exchange (2010) is 6.4 million dollars, or almost 100 times that of the average worker. Also, it found that, since 2001, the base pay for executives in Australia had risen by 130%, while average weekly earnings had risen by 52%. However, average weekly earnings for full-time adults only increased by 5.2% in one year[97].

According to the Australian Financial Review's 13th annual survey of executive salaries, the total packages of CEOs of the top 300 listed companies rose 4% to an average of US$2.33 million, with an estimated CEO-to-worker pay ratio of 100:1. Similarly, research by the Australian Council of Superannuation Investors shows that top 100 CEO pay has outstripped shareholder returns by more than three times. According to the Australian Council of Trade Unions, the average total remuneration of a CEO of a top 50 company listed on the Australian Securities Exchange in 2010 is US$6.4 million. The average CEO's total pay package is now worth almost 100 times that of the average worker.

Executive pay rose by an average of over US$940,000 over the past year, the equivalent of an extra US$18,000 a week, while the annual wage for a full-time worker rose by just US$3200 or US$62 per week. The estimated GINI for Australia is 0.30, while GDP is at around US$1.5 trillion.

New Zealand

In New Zealand, according to a study published in June 2012, the value of the average CEO pay package dropped in 2011, by 0.4%. According to Statistics NZ, the mean weekly income for all New Zealanders rose 2.5% in the year to the June 2011 quarter, while CEOs had an average pay of US$1.5 million. Between 2004 and 2010, the average CEO pay package ballooned by almost 80%. Over the same period, the average worker's earnings rose 27% from US$33,800 to almost US$43,000. The CEO and Top Executives survey and Directors' Fees survey estimates that in general, base salaries for CEOs have been on the rise with median base salaries for CEOs up by nearly 10%.

According to a report by the Inequality blog, New Zealand suffers from a large income gap. In fact, from 1980 to 2008,

New Zealand's top 1% captured 20% of total income growth, according to a presentation by OECD's Michael Forster at a conference entitled "Increasing Inequality: Causes, Consequences and Responses". The OECD analysis showed that technological change and increasing rewards for skilled workers played a big part in increasing inequality, as well as other factors.

The CEO-to-worker pay ratio was estimated to be at 37:1, while the average salary is estimated to be US$43,000. Adult minimum wage earners get US$27,000 per year and the average annual pay of the heads of NZ's listed companies was US$1.6 million per year. Average workers' earnings were US$43,000 per year.

The country's GINI index was estimated to be at 0.362, while the GDP was estimated to be US$172 billion.

FACT: SINCE 2001, BASE PAY FOR EXECUTIVES IN AUSTRALIA ROSE BY 130%, WHILE THE AVERAGE EMPLOYEE ONLY GOT A 5.2% BUMP.

EUROPE

In Europe, the President of the European Commission's (EC) Eurogroup of Finance Ministers, Jean-Claude Juncker, called excessive pay a "social scourge" and demanded action. In the UK, executive compensation has also caused public upset.

In the meantime, the European Union has already taken a big step towards putting strict limits on the bonuses paid to bankers. If the measure, which is still opposed by the UK government, becomes European law, the bonuses that many bankers receive would be capped at no more than equal to their annual salaries, starting next year. Only if a bank's shareholders approved could a bonus be higher, and even then it would be limited to no more than double the salary.

The move is part of a package of banking regulations known as Basel III and is aimed at reducing the danger of big bank failures, but a majority of the EU's 27 members would need to approve the rules for them to take effect. The agreement is a potential blow on Britain as its economy partly relies on generous remuneration packages.

The limits on bonuses would also apply to bankers employed by EU banks but working outside the bloc. The EU authorities are drafting separate rules that could restrict remuneration at private equity firms and hedge funds. The law is intended to reduce the financial incentives that led bankers to take risky bets, like those made on subprime housing debt in the US during the credit bubble, but some critics have warned that institutions might defeat the intent of the legislation by raising bankers' base pay. Also, some bankers said the rule posed the question of why the bonus cap would not apply to other industries where staff members stand to gain large bonus.

FACT: IN 2008, EUROGROUP CHAIRMAN JEAN-CLAUDE JUNCKER CALLED COMPENSATION EXCESSES "SCANDAL" AND "SOCIAL SCOURGE".

UNITED KINGDOM (UK)

In 2011, the Compass organisation described executive pay as "corrosive" and in December 2011/January 2012, two of the country's biggest investors, Fidelity Worldwide Investment and the Association of British Insurers, called for greater shareholder control over executive pay packages.

According to a study by the Heritage Institute[98], the average CEO compensation as a multiple of average employee compensation was of 25 times more the worker's average pay in 2000. However, a different study puts UK CEO remuneration at 145 times higher than average worker compensation. According to a study by the Paris School of Economics, a typical FTSE 100 executive enjoys a pay package of £3.75 million, 145 times more than their workers (The High Pay Commission). In 1999, the boss typically earned 69 times their worker's salary. By 2007, it peaked at 161 times.

According to data by the High Pay Commission, the average salary in the UK is at £25,816, while the GINI index was estimated to be at 0.34 and the GDP, US$2.5 trillion[99].

SWITZERLAND

Switzerland seemed to be in the forefront of the run to end the widening gap between CEO and employee pay, but its efforts to regulate CEO pay have so far failed. It looked like the referendum to deal with "abusive remuneration" would have been approved – the Minder initiative, to reinforce the rights of shareholders to prevent high salaries and bonuses, determining the duration of the mandate of the members of the boards to one year and prohibiting certain forms of remuneration, like "millionaire" compensation or bonuses from the acquisition of companies[100].

Thomas Minder started the fight against abusive remunerations in 2004. He opposes to the boards assigning astronomic salaries to board members instead of dividends to shareholders. In addition, due to the continued widening of the wage gap in Switzerland, two popular initiatives have been launched in response to public outrage. This happened after it became public that the lowest-paid employee at the pharmaceutical company Novartis would have to work 266 years to earn the US$17.1 million the company's CEO Joseph Jimenez received in 2011, the largest wage differential measured by the trade union group Travail Suisse in its annual survey. The Chairman of Novartis came third with a ratio of one to 229 in 2011, heading the ranking of top earners between 2005 and 2009, only to be dethroned by Credit Suisse head Brady Dougan who earned 1,812 times more than the lowest paid employees at the Swiss bank.

Over the past two years, the wage gap has narrowed slightly, according to the trade union Unia, which calculated that in 2011, a top manager earned about 39 times more than an entry-level employee did, down from 43 times in 2010. However, this decrease is minor when compared to the profits of the top 41 public companies, which plunged 35%.

At the time of the announcement, Fribourg University professor Jean-Jacques Friboulet told swissinfo.ch: "There is no economic justification for exorbitant executive salaries"[101]. According to the professor, evolution has shown that economy cannot regulate itself, and that is why he supports an initiative "against rip-off salaries" to be voted on by the Swiss electorate in March. If accepted, shareholders will be asked to approve the pay of public companies' executives and board members". The initiative demands the introduction of a new article in the constitution comprising a number of measures to strengthen shareholder rights, with the main goal of making sure that executives of public companies cannot pay themselves excessive remuneration which does not bear any relationship to financial results.

Thus the initiative gives shareholders the right to elect all the board members at the annual general meeting and they can also decide on the amount of remuneration for the directors, executives and members of the advisory board. Upfront payments, termination pay and bonuses when companies are bought or sold are forbidden. Proxy voting is also not allowed. If the initiative is rejected in March, the counterproposal will come into force: a revision of the law on stock companies and the financial reporting act, incorporating some of the proposed measures, but only in a limited form. According to Friboulet, a scale of one to 12 is acceptable in the public sector, but does not fit well in the private industry because "market economics only works if a company can attract executives".

On November 24, 2013, the Swiss voted in a referendum on whether to enshrine the 1:12 pay ratio -- in their national constitution, no less. The initiative was backed by an assortment of mainstream political groups, who argue that CEO pay in Switzerland has gotten out of hand and needs to be reined in. According to the groups, the ratio of top to bottom earners in Swiss firms has grown from about 1 to 6 in 1984 to 1 to 43 today, and that is only the average as the gap is much wider in banks.

The top 100 Swiss companies, boasting household names like Glencore, Nestlé, Novartis, Roche, ABB, Adecco, Migros, Holcim, Cargill International SA, Coop, Kühne + Nagel, Mercuria Energy Trading, Syngenta and Xstrata, found it difficult to accept such a massive paradigm shift and they were satisfied with the outcome, as Swiss voters rejected the proposal.

Overall, the measure was opposed by 65% of voters. This does not come as a surprise, as Switzerland is the home to at least five of Europe's 20 best-paid CEOs. However, polls had suggested the initiative could pass. Minister of Economy Johann Schneider-Ammann, welcomed the decision, classifying pay curbs as "absurd" and welcoming the voters' decision. "We know there would have been lots of ways to circumvent the restrictions", he said. "Switzerland stays attractive as a business location".

FACT: SWITZERLAND IS ONE OF THE PIONEERS IN THE RACE TO CURB INCOME INEQUALITY.

FRANCE

In France, the fight against abusive salaries is also undergoing. The country announced in May 2012 it will cap the salaries of CEOs at state-owned companies, signalling a pay cut for EDF's Henri Proglio. Salaries for the heads of state companies will be limited to 20 times the company's lowest paid worker. The measure would apply to existing contracts and call upon the "patriotism" of corporate leaders in the face of the economic crisis.

The Finance Minister announced in May 2013 that the government was no longer planning to cap executives' salaries in the private sector, following a move, which made it look like France was following the steps of Switzerland. Not too far, however, as concerns that the measure would antagonise the big businesses needed to reinvigorate the economy quickly made the government change its mind. The Socialist government had imposed limits in 2012 on executive pay at state-run companies and had pledged to do the same in the private sector. "There will be no specific draft law on the governance of companies", Minister Pierre Moscovici was quoted as saying in an interview with business daily *Les Echos*[102].

The CEO-to-worker pay ratio in France was estimated to be at 23:1, with French private sector employees earning an average US$30,948. In 2010, the average salary for CEOs was US$1.7 million. The GINI Index for France was estimated to be at around 0.32, while the GDP is approximately US$2.77 trillion.

FACT: IN FRANCE, THE 20:1 CAMPAIGN WAS ABANDONED OUT OF FEAR OF SCARING AWAY THE BIG SPENDERS.

Spain

In Spain, the government has renewed its crackdown on executive pay in state companies as it obliges senior managers to share the pain of austerity. It announced that basic annual salaries at state-owned firms would be limited to 105,000 Euros, though it has left room for government-approved productivity bonuses. This would cut the average CEO salary by up to 35% at about 4,000 state-owned and partly state-owned firms.

The CEO-to-worker pay ratio was calculated at 17:1, with an average salary of US$28,856 per year and a GINI index of 0.32, while the GDP is of approximately US$1.47 trillion.

Following Switzerland's footsteps, the opposition Social Democrats have just adopted the 1:12 campaign as their official policy.

Portugal

According to a study from 2011 undertaken by the Portuguese watchdog DECO[103], CEO compensation sometimes represents 100 times the average salary in large companies. According to data from 2009, the salary of the CEO is approximately 37 times higher than the average salary of the company's workers. On average, the executive leader of national companies earned more than 800,000 euros in 2009.

In a general manner, the smaller companies have a smaller CEO-to-worker ratio. In public companies, big disparities were found between the average salaries and the CEO pay.

The current crisis has in fact led to a reduction in base pay, but executives have managed to bypass this with their bonuses. According to the study, executives receive nearly four times their salary in bonuses.

The average salary was estimated to be at US$27,775, while CEO's get on average US$1 million per year, and the GINI index was estimated to be at 0.385, while the GDP was calculated at US$237 billion.

NORWAY

In Norway, executive pay is considered modest – even low – when compared to other countries. According to a report by Aftenposten[104], new figures from pension, finance and life insurance agency KLP, along with academic estimates, show that Norwegian CEOs earn roughly 16 times the incomes of "average workers". Executive pay has increased more than the average raises granted to Norwegian workers over the past 20 years, but executive salaries are still small when compared to other countries.

According to Iver Braglien, a professor at Norwegian business school NHH in Bergen, the lower executive pay levels in Norway are attributed to the country's "social democratic culture and egalitarian thinking", which attempts to narrow differences in wealth within the population.

A different report published in 2009 puts the ratio at 4:1, which corresponds to a tenth of what US top executive colleagues earn. The average salary for CEOs in Norway was estimated to be at US$526,287, while the GINI index was calculated to be at 0.258 and the GDP at US$485 billion.

SWEDEN

Similarly, in Sweden, highly paid executives also make much less than their US and UK counterparts, albeit delivering strong corporate results. In fact, executives in Sweden generally get far less than the ones in the rest of Europe and appear to perform just as well – or better.

According to a study by the Hay Group[105], the purchasing power of Swedish executives ranked second-lowest in the OECD, while 2007 Eurostat data put average pay for Swedish managers and senior officials about 20% below their UK counterparts.

Still, CEO-to-worker pay ratio was estimated to be at 19:1, with an average salary of USD 2,886 per month. According to a review by Hallvarsson & Halvarsson (H&H) carried out in 2009, the variable compensation paid to Swedish CEOs is much lower than that paid to CEOs in other countries. The heads of Sweden's 23 largest listed companies earn an average of US$1.87 million per year. The GINI index was calculated at 0.25, while the GDP was estimated to be US$539 billion.

SOUTH AFRICA

South Africa has also recently started discussing the pay gap between top management and workers as being the key driver of the country's labour market instability and the reason for the rise in unprotected strikes, with the number of man-days lost due to strikes averaging 3-4 million per year for the last two decades[106].

According to a Nedbank Private Wealth political analyst JP Landman, cited by Business Day, inequality is the key driver of labour action. "Most people would agree that inequality is a serious issue in this country"[107], he said. "We can expect severe tensions in our body politics in future years".

A study by management consultants P-E Corporate Services[108] said that CEOs earned up to 52 times more than their most junior staff last year, which seems to be the fact at the core of worker dissatisfaction. "It comes down to comparison – workers look at what CEOs get and what they get. South Africa is one of the most unequal countries in the world", he explained[109]. Thinking about the current unemployment market across the world, relativity is not enough to explain employee satisfaction. In our current society, due to the control of the media, valuable professionals are not the ones that generate the most economic value, nor are they the most skilled.

Executive pay at mining companies has been one of the main issues, with South African fund managers overseeing almost US$180 billion in assets saying they are stepping up pressure on mining companies to curb executive pay as return to shareholder dwindle, in a Bloomberg report. "Costs are going up double-digit, money is not coming in, yet we are seeing a big, big rise in executive pay", Fidelis Madavo, who helps manage about US$140 billion at Public Investment Corp., South Africa's state pension fund, said at a conference in Johannesburg. "We have been talking to CEOs individually on this", he told Bloomberg.

Over 2002-2012, pay for CEOs at South African mining companies increased 12-fold while dividends dropped 25%, according to a presentation by Michael Schroder, a fund manager at Old Mutual Plc. "We are not happy", he said. "Something clearly has gone wrong here"[110].

In fact, CEOs of companies on the Johannesburg Stock Exchange are paid an average 54 times more than the lowest-earning worker at their companies, according to a study published by PricewaterhouseCoopers LLP. Investors are starting to be heard by mining companies' boards and fund managers expect compensation packages to drop in the next few years.

Sandy McGregor, a fund manager at Allan Gray Ltd, told Bloomberg: "There are a lot of executives in the mining industry who are getting more than they should. We don't mind people getting very large remuneration packages, but they must have done something to deserve it". Old Mutual's Schroder said: "My advice to the CEOs is this: Your personal greed is the biggest obstacle for the turn of this trend".

The CEO-to-worker pay ratio estimated for South Africa is of 51:1, according to a study by the Heritage Institute relating to 2000. Despite the economic downturn in 2008, CEOs were still able to double their earnings. "In 2009, the average salary of a CEO was 4.8 million... that is 36 times more than the average worker".

The average salary estimated in the country is of US$13,330, with a GINI index of 0.631 in 2009, according to a World Bank report published in 2010. The GDP was calculated at US$408 billion.

MYTH: CEO compensation is calculated according to the performance of the executive and the company...

CHINA

In China, CEO pay is relatively low when compared to that in developed countries. However, there is a tremendous pay gap in this country: China's official labour force of around 795 million equates 59% of the population. Out of the 795 million, only 28.7% are in industry (228 million, or 17% of the population). Considering the European Union (EU) has a total labour force of 228 million, and the US 154.9 million, we get some 'food for thought'.

On average, Chinese manufacturing workers are estimated to earn US$0.52 per hour.

The CEO-to-worker pay ratio was estimated to be at 20:1 in China, with a GINI index of 0.474 and a GDP of US$8.358 trillion in 2012.

FACT: ALTHOUGH CEO PAY IS RELATIVELY LOW IN CHINA, THE PAY GAP IS ONE OF THE HIGHEST.

BRAZIL

In 2001, Brazil ranked as the world's most unequal major nation, with its 10% most affluent people grabbing nearly 50 times more income, on average, than the nation's poorest tenth, over double the US gap, according to a report by The New York Times. In terms of the GINI Index, the World Bank's databank[111] shows that Brazil registered an index of 52.7 in 2010-2014.

The CEO-to-worker pay ratio was estimated to be 57:1, after salaries of CEOs from Brazilian companies increased by 10% from 2009 to 2010. According to a study by Catho Online, the average salary of Brazilian CEOs went from R$43,669 (US$22,021.66) to R$48,215 (US$24,314, annually, that would be US$291,768) between October 2008 and October 2009. According to a study by Mercer, in 2013, companies intend to give their CEOs a raise of 8%.

MYTH: In the US, the work of top CEOs is more than 200 times more valuable than that of regular company employees

Brazil's Institute of Geography and Statistics (IBGE)[112] estimates that the country's overall average monthly salary is US$678.90 (US$8,146.8 per year). According to Payscale, a worker with a Bachelor's degree will have an average salary between R$54,431 and R$166,979 (US$27,448 and US$84,205). According to World Bank estimates, Brazil's GDP was at US$2,476 billion

FACT: BRAZIL IS AMONG THE WORLD'S MOST UNEQUAL COUNTRIES: ITS 10% RICHEST HAVE 50% MORE THAN THE COUNTRY'S POOREST TENTH.

PARADOX: Company profits are dropping and the economy is weaker than ever, but CEO compensation continues to rise...

JAPAN

In Japan, CEOs also earn less than in their Western counterparts. However, many Western investors argue that Japanese executives get paid too little and that performance should be a bigger factor in determining compensation packages.

In 2010, companies in Japan were forced to disclose top executives' pay as the country's financial regulator aims to increase corporate governance over a compensation system that is based on seniority and not performance.

CEO-to-worker pay ratio was estimated to be at around 16:1, while the average salary was US$580,000 for CEOs and the GINI index, 0.381. The GDP was US$5,870 billion

IDEA: Executive compensation needs to be regulated in order to accurately reflect the performance of the company and the individual.

GLOBAL PROBLEM

This chapter aims to identify the main issues that lead to global income inequality and assess the negative impact this has over the economy, namely, in terms of employee dissatisfaction and the loss of motivation, which ultimately lead to a weaker performance. Finally, it aims to identify the most recent measures taken to fight this inequality and define expectations for the future.

It includes the following observations: (1) Speculation is at the Root of Inequality; (2) Inequality Negatively Impacts Performance and (3) The Situation could be Changing.

All of these observations follow extensive research on the causes of inequality as well as the presentation of the reasons why we believe that speculation is negatively affecting the economy and the positive signs that prove there are efforts towards an improving situation.

OUR MAIN CONCERN IS THE IDENTIFICATION OF PROBLEMATIC AREAS WHEN IT COMES TO INEQUALITY AND THE PROVISION OF A CLEAR EXPLANATION, AS WELL AS SEEKING SIGNS OF RECOVERY/IMPROVEMENT.

OBSERVATION: SPECULATION IS AT THE ROOT OF INEQUALITY

"All money is a matter of belief." – Adam Smith

"It is well enough that people of the nation do not understand our banking and monetary system, for if they did, I believe there would be a revolution before tomorrow morning." – Henry Ford

We are living beyond our means… and we have to get our act together." – Nouriel Roubini

"International lending banks need to focus on areas where private investment doesn't go, such as infrastructure projects, education and poverty relief." – Joseph E. Stiglitz

"I recognized that information was, in many respects, like a public good, and it was this insight that made it clear to me that it was unlikely that the private market would provide efficient resource allocations whenever information was endogenous." – Joseph E. Stiglitz

"The same is true for the market economy: the power of markets is enormous, but they have no inherent moral character. We have to decide how to manage them… For all these reasons, it is plain that markets must be tamed and tempered to make sure they work to the benefit of most citizens. And that has to be done repeatedly, to ensure that they continue to do so." – Joseph E. Stiglitz

"Excessive leverage has large societal costs," he said in prepared testimony. "Banks, and especially the big banks, need to be restrained." – Joseph E. Stiglitz

It is surprising that the first stock exchange thrived for years without a single stock being traded. In fact, the origin of the concept of the stock exchange goes back as far as the 1300s, with Europe's moneylenders who traded debts between each other. With the evolution of their business, the lenders began to sell debt issues to costumers – the first investors. Venetians hold the title of the leaders in this field and were the first to start trading the securities from other governments.

FACT: When the New York Stock Exchange was created, there was no paper money changing hands or even the idea of stocks. Rather, they traded silver for papers saying they owned shares in cargo that was coming in on ships every day. The trade flourished.

However, the first stock exchange opened in Antwerp, Belgium, in 1531. Here, brokers and moneylenders would meet to deal in business, government and individual debt issues. In fact, there were no real stocks in the 1500s. Thus, no official share that changed hands. Later on, in the 1600s, Dutch, British and French government gave charters to companies with East India in their names. To lessen the risk of ship voyages, ship owners used investors who would put up money for the voyage in return for a percentage of the proceeds. Here, companies were already paying dividends on the proceeds.

The British East India Company had one of the biggest competitive advantages in financial history – a government-backed monopoly. Then when investors began receiving dividends and started selling their shares, others wanted to take part. That gave rise to the South Seas Company (SSC) in England, with a similar charter and issues were sold as soon as they were listed. Encouraged by the success of the SSC, other businessmen rushed to offer new shares in their own ventures. Inevitably, the bubble burst when the SSC failed to pay any dividends due to its insufficient profits.

PARADOX: Savings can be harmful to the economy (s. Paradox of Thrift by Keynes)

In London, the first stock exchange was formed in 1773, 19 years before the New York Stock Exchange. While the first was handcuffed by the law that restricted shares, the NYSE has dealt in the trading of stocks since its inception. Currently, the New York Stock Exchange has billions of dollars changing hands every day and thousands of companies being traded, affecting millions of people. This is very different from its early days, when there was no paper money changing hands or even the idea of stocks. Rather, they traded silver for papers saying they owned shares in cargo coming in on ships every day, and this led trade to flourish.

In fact, the role of the New York Stock Market progressed during the American Revolution, when the government needed money to fund its wartime operations. One way they did this was by selling bonds – pieces of paper a person buys for a set price, knowing that after a certain period of time, they can exchange them for profit. In addition, the first banks in the country started selling parts or shares of their own companies to people in order to raise money. Basically, they would sell part of the company to whoever wanted to buy it – the essence of the modern day stock market.

On the international scene, London emerged as the major exchange hub in Europe, but many companies that were able to list internationally still listed in New York. Many other countries developed their own stock exchanges, but these were largely seen as training grounds before they were ready to make the leap to the LSE and then the NYSE.

In fact, nowadays, the NYSE remains the largest and most powerful stock exchange in the world, with a market capitalisation that is larger than Tokyo, London and the Nasdaq combined. It has become a truly global stock exchange and thus one of the key elements when it comes to speculation and, consequently, its relation with market movements and the performance of companies themselves.

FRACTIONAL RESERVE

Another concept highly associated with speculation and one of the most recent "paradoxes" in the US, is the fractional reserve[113], a banking system also known as "fractional deposit lending", in which only a fraction of bank deposits are backed by actual cash-on-hand and are available for withdrawal. This is done to expand the economy by freeing up capital that can be loaned out to other parties, Investopedia explains. This is a highly risk method, which was made obvious by the time when, during the Great Depression, many US banks were forced to shut down because so many people tried to withdraw assets at the same time. Although the method is a bit more safeguarded these days, it still remains in place.

In 1935, economist Irving Fisher[114] proposed a system of 100% reserve banking as a means of reversing the deflation of the Great Depression. He wrote: "100 per cent banking [...] would give the Federal Reserve absolute control over the money supply. Recall that under the present fractional reserve system of depository institutions, the money supply is determined in the short run by such non-policy variables as the currency/deposit ratio of the public and the excess reserve ratio of depository institutions."

IDEA: Full transparency in all central bank decisions

Milton Friedman said: "Our present fractional reserve banking system has two major defects. First, it involves extensive governmental intervention into lending and investing activities that should preferably be left to the free market. Second, decisions by holders of money about the form in which they want to hold money and by banks about the structure of their assets tend to affect the amount available to lend. This has often been referred to as the 'inherent instability' of a fractional reserve system".

FACT: DECISIONS BY MONEY HOLDERS ABOUT HOW TO HOLD THE MONEY AND DECISIONS BY BANKS ABOUT THE STRUCTURE OF THEIR ASSETS AFFECT THE AMOUNT AVAILABLE TO LEND.

THE CAPITAL MARKET

The capital market and leverage also go hand-in-hand with speculation and have also been highly associated with inequality. Trading in high prices, which appear to be based on implausible or inconsistent expectations shows that decisions are mostly made based on uncertainty and speculation, or even price coordination or any other type of agreements.

A few theories have been developed regarding the use of intrinsic values, namely the "Greater Fool Theory", which stipulates that bubbles are driven by the behaviour of optimistic market participants who buy overvalued assets in anticipation of selling it to other speculators at a much higher price. Moreover, extrapolation, or the projection of historical data into the future, on the basis that, if prices have risen at a certain rate in the past, they will continue to do so. This has led investors to overbid on risk assets to continue capturing the same rates of return. Moreover, the concept of "herding", or the fact that, investors tend to buy or sell in the direction of the market trend. Finally, "moral hazard", the prospect that a party insulated from risk may behave differently from the way it would behave if fully exposed to risk – the risk-return relationship.

Therefore, it seems obvious that the capital market strongly revolves around decisions based on virtual assets and virtual performances, and so is CEO compensation: executives are compensated by short-term speculative decisions on assets that do not belong to them – and in fact, assets that are not real!

FACT: THE CAPITAL MARKET, ORIGINALLY DEVELOPED TO HELP FIRMS OBTAIN FUNDING, IS NOW ASSOCIATED WITH SPECULATION.

CARTELS

Cartels[115] are another key element when talking about inequality, mainly because they represent the concentration and abuse of power[116]. These are organisations created from a formal agreement between a group of producers of a good or service to regulate supply in an effort to regulate or manipulate prices, acting as a single producer to influence prices by controlling production and marketing. These organisations and their manipulations are well-known, albeit prohibited, in most countries. Although having less command over an industry than a monopoly where a single group or company owns all or nearly all of a given product or service's market, they are widely chosen as a way of controlling industries and sectors.

Although cartels are illegal in the United States, for instance, the Organisation of Petroleum Exporting Countries (OPEC) is protected by US foreign trade laws and represents the largest cartel in the world. Amid controversy in the mid-2000s, the US Congress attempted to penalise OPEC as an illegal cartel, but the effort was blocked over concerns of retaliation and potential negative effects on US businesses.

In a study entitled *International Cartels*[117] published in *Issues in Competition Law and Policy*, Levenstein and Suslow prove that, despite strong antitrust laws against price fixing in most countries and increasingly strong enforcement, international cartels continue to operate and have been uncovered in the past years in a wide range of goods and services. According to the article, the cartels that survive the longest do so by investing in elaborate communication and information-sharing mechanisms, which reduce uncertainty and help the cartels escape from the Prisoner's Dilemma that undermines cartel stability.

The Prisoner's Dilemma is an example of a game analysed in game theory that shows why two individuals might not cooperate, even if it appears that it is in their best interests to do so. The game was formalised as follows by Albert W. Tucker:

Two members of a criminal gang are arrested and imprisoned. Each prisoner is in solitary confinement with no means of speaking to or exchanging messages with the other. The police admit they don't have enough evidence to convict the pair on the principal charge. They plan to sentence both to a year in prison on a lesser charge. Simultaneously, the police offer each prisoner a Faustian bargain. Each prisoner is given the opportunity either to betray the other, by testifying that the other committed the crime, or to cooperate with the other by remaining silent. It is implied that the prisoners will have no opportunity to reward or punish their partner other than the prison sentences they get, and that their decision will not affect their reputation in the future.

Because betraying a partner offers a greater reward than cooperating with them, all purely rational self-interested prisoners would betray the other, and so the only possible outcome for two rational prisoners is for them to betray each other. The interesting part of the result is that pursuing individual reward logically leads both of the prisoners to betray, when they would get a better reward if they both cooperated.

The prisoner's dilemma game can be used as a model for many real world situations involving cooperative behaviour, applied to situations not strictly matching the formal criteria of the classic games. For example, those in which two entities could gain important benefits from cooperating or suffer from the failure to do so, but find it difficult or expensive, or necessarily impossible, to coordinate their activities to achieve cooperation.

DO WE NEED PROMOTIONS?

However, to escape from this dilemma, cartels tend to use elaborate compensation schemes to deter cheating without resorting to expensive and destabilising price wars. Although these cartels do have a limited life, they have the potential to cause significant harm to consumers, via increased prices, and significant harm to the nature of competition in the marketplace, if the cartel successfully impedes entry.

HIGH-SPEED TRADING

High-speed trading, or High-Frequency Trading (HFT) is a programme trading platform that uses powerful computers to transact a large number of orders at very fast speeds. It uses complex algorithms to analyse multiple markets and execute orders based on market conditions. As of 2012, it was estimated that more than 50% of exchange volume came from HFT orders[118].

HFT became popular when exchanges began to offer incentives for companies to add liquidity to the market. For instance, the NYSE has a group of liquidity providers called supplemental liquidity providers (SLPs) which attempt to add competition and liquidity for existing quotes on the exchange. As an incentive to the firm, the NYSE pays a fee or rebate for providing the said liquidity. The SLP was introduced following the collapse of Lehman Brothers in 2008, when liquidity was a major concern for investors.

Earlier last year, in March 2014, the FBI started probing whether HFT firms are engaging in insider trading by taking advantage of fast-moving market information unavailable to other investors, according to an article by the WSJ. The probe follows heightened scrutiny of computerised trading and for the FBI, this investigation marks a new and unusual phase of its focus on insider trading.

For the Columbia University Professor and Nobel laureate Joseph Stiglitz[119], HFT gives an unfair advantage to a selected group of investors and could be taxed as a way to discourage the practice. It results in "sophisticated versions of front-running" and "has resulted in an unlevelled playing field", he told Bloomberg. "It is mostly a zero sum game – or more accurately, a negative sum game because it costs real resources to win in this game", he added.

IDEA: Ban short-selling, high speed trading and all other instruments of pure speculation

In 2011, the International Monetary Fund (IMF) launched a conference entitled "Macro and Growth Policies in the Wake of the Crisis". The four post-conference posts laid out by Michael Spence[120], former Stanford School of Business dean and winner of the 2001 Nobel Memorial Prize in Economic Sciences, he explained why HFTs should be totally banned. "I would ban high speed trading – the automated, computer-driven trading of large volumes of financial assets in a short timeframe", he said, "by introducing lags in the trading process or increasing capital requirements or both". According to Spence this is "a zero-sum game, using resources, contributing potential volatility in markets". "The economic benefits in terms of enhancing the pricing, capital allocation and risk spreading functions of the financial system, seem negligible", he concluded.

According to Spence, one of the key elements in financial regulation is restricting excessive leverage, namely in banks. "Regulating the shadow banking system is crucial", he says. Additionally, he states that the current structure of the financial system "is shot through with actual and potential conflicts of interest", which have a negative impact on incentives and performance "and perhaps more importantly, trust"[121].

Short selling has also been a target of much polemic across the corporate world. It consists on a way of profiting from a fall in a company's share price[122]. In other words, selling a share you do not own to buy it back once the price has fallen, netting a profit in the process. When it goes according to plan, the investor pays less to buy back the shares than it receives for selling them. However, short selling has often been associated with market abuse. In an article on *The Independent* entitled 'The Big Question: What is short selling, and is it a practice that should be stamped out?', HBOS is given as an example of a company that has severely suffered from short selling. Earlier in 2015, its shares plunged when rumours swept the stock market that the bank had financial problems. The rumours were false and the share price recovered later that day, but in the meantime, investors with short positions in HBOS shares had made a gain. There is widespread suspicion that the rumours were planted by a hedge fund keen to make a fast buck, but this has been difficult to investigate.

To resolve this issue, regulators have tried to police short selling. In the US, for example, the SEC has prosecuted traders for spreading false rumours about companies that they have sold short. In the meantime, new rules have also been introduced and pressure has been brought to bear on stock lenders, but short selling remains a legitimate investment practice and an outright ban would be a draconian intervention.

The economist Joseph Stiglitz has been one of the biggest critics of inequality and speculation. He believes that "inequality between countries is far greater than inequality within countries". According to Stiglitz, "average global incomes, by country, have moved closer together over the last several decades, particularly on the strength of the growth of China and India. But overall equality across humanity, considered as individuals, has improved very little". He goes on to say that while emerging countries are now catching up with the West, "the poor everywhere are left behind, even in places like China where they have benefited somewhat from rising living standards".

To illustrate this, he cites World Bank economist Brank Milanovic, who said that "people in the world's top 1% saw their incomes increase by 60%, while those in the bottom 5% had no change in their income. And while median incomes have greatly improved in recent decades, there are still enormous imbalances: 8% of humanity takes home 50% of global income; the top 1% alone takes home 15%".

Stiglitz sees inequality as dramatically changed over the years[123]. While recently disclosed census figures reveal that median income in America has not changed in almost a quarter of a century, the top 1% of Americans took home 22% of the nation's income in 2012. In fact, 95% of all income gains since 2009 have gone to the top 1%. Right now, the typical American makes less than he did 45 years ago and people who graduated from high school but do not have a college degree make almost 40% less than they did four decades ago.

In Europe, the situation is going a similar way. Rising austerity is leading to high unemployment rates, falling wages and increasing inequality. Stiglitz believes that although the German chancellor Angela Merkel and Mario Draghi, the president of the European Central Bank, blame this on bloated welfare spending, this line of thought has only immerged Europe further into recession. "On both sides of the Atlantic, the austerity fanatics say, march on: these are the bitter pills that we need to take to achieve prosperity. But prosperity for whom?" he argues.

"On both sides of the Atlantic, the austerity fanatics say, march on: these are the bitter pills that we need to take to achieve prosperity. But prosperity for whom?" – Stiglitz

Stiglitz blames the situation on excessive financialisation – weak corporate governance, eroding social cohesion and asymmetric globalisation – workers make wage concessions and governments make tax concessions. "The result is a race to the bottom", he states. He concludes: "For these reasons, I see us entering a world divided not just between the haves and have-nots, but also between those countries that do nothing about it, and those that do". According to Stiglitz, while some countries will be able to create a shared prosperity (the only type of prosperity he believes is truly sustainable), "others will let inequality run amok".

THE FINANCIAL INDUSTRY IS TO BLAME

So it comes as no surprise that the financial industry is where we find a more disproportionate CEO-to-worker ratio. Also, there does not seem to be any accountability for results at the core of this industry: executives are compensated by their successes and the transactions they perform, regardless of the outcomes being positive or negative. They are never penalised when the results are negative, so what is there to lose?

We could thus characterise the capital market as a sort of house of speculation – basically, a betting house – which is now distanced from its original function, which was to enable companies to get capital from investors.

MYTH: Stocks that go up must come down (and vice versa)

This means markets are now dominated by large funds, which are in turn controlled by executives who take no responsibility for their actions and decisions. On the other hand, the concept of the stock market does not take into consideration the impact that technology has on it, since it was designed for a paper world, and not a virtual world, with a completely different aim.

"We don't live in a free market society... markets are controlled by the major players who influence legislation to perpetuate their control"

Instead of providing capital to companies – the original objective of the capital market – these practices enable and encourage movements based on speculation, always controlled by the same so-called "giants". The other players can be described as surfers, merely waiting to catch the next set of waves. The waves are created by the "giants" who dominate the markets, and who also control the large funds.

"The capital market and indexes have become a gambling vehicle." – Warren Buffet.

In the words of the American business magnate Warren Buffett, the capital market has turned into "a gambling vehicle". "Gambling involves, in my view, the creation of a risk where no risk needs to be created", he explained. "Now, obviously, if you plant a crop in the spring and you're going to harvest in the fall, you are speculating on what prices are going to be in the fall for your corn or oats or whatever it may be. And you may lay that off on some other speculator", he added. "But that's a risk that the system has to take. You can't grow it in one day. But when you start wagering on – well, on stock index futures, I think that gambling instincts are very strong on humans."

IDEA: Performance needs to be easily quantifiable to lead to fair rewards and should be linked to objective results, not virtual results that could be associated with speculation.

IDEA: Monitor, transparently, and enforce the separation of Democracy powers: Legislative; Executive; Judicial

OBSERVATION: INEQUALITY NEGATIVELY IMPACTS PERFORMANCE

Economy Nobel Prize winners Paul Krugman and Stiglitz, have both been fierce debaters of the role of inequality and its impact across the world. Both argue it can damage firms and even the economy as a whole, as it diverts workers' efforts from jobs that are difficult to measure, but are nevertheless highly important, and by over-incentivising the easily measured aspects of performance.

According to experiments undertaken with asset markets, short-term bonuses can contribute to price bubbles, which is consistent with the theory that inequality contributes to economic crashes. German economist Eckhard Hein suggests these incentives "have imposed short-termism on management", which he believes has led to a preference for financial investment, "generating high profits in the short-run", in detriment to "real investment in capital stock and long-run growth".

FACT: "OVERLY HIGH COMPENSATION PAID TO CEOS HAS IMPOSED A DECREASE IN MANAGEMENT'S 'ANIMAL SPIRITS' AND AN INCREASE IN THE PREFERENCE FOR FINANCIAL INVESTMENT" – ECKHARD HEIN

As well as highly affecting economic performance, it has been proven that inequality affects microeconomic firm-specific channels, eroding work ethics. Overall, it is important to note that the concept of inequality has changed. It is no longer seen as an outcome of the equilibrium of an economy, but because of wealth distribution, which is now highly influenced by the capital market.

PARADOX: Achieving a better life than the last generations becomes elusive in countries where the gap between rich and poor is larger.

IMPACT ON PERFORMANCE

Funded by the European Fifth Framework Programme, London School of Economics' (LSE) David Marsden, who is project coordinator for the project report on *Pay Inequalities and Economic Performance*[124], brought about what could be seen as a confusing perspective. He argues that greater pay inequalities within firms appear to be related to better business performance. Nevertheless, he reached the conclusion that as levels of inequality increase, the relationship appears to decline and the incentive effect appears to depend on the type of work organisation and human resource management approach adopted by the firm. Therefore, pay inequality only benefits corporate performance, when it reaches a "healthy" level, which can lead employees to work better, aspiring to reach the top.

Not only does this inequality affect performance throughout a company, but it also affects the business mind of entrepreneurs. At the World 12th HR Congress, Charles Handy stated that in the banking sector now, we see that "people are beginning to say business is selfish". He continues: "Business, they feel, is only interested in getting richer, both corporately and individually and in growth. But we are not here to make as much money as possible; we are here to do our job for society". According to Handy, in this climate, many people inside organisations are not happy. In fact, a survey in the UK revealed that 72% did not like their organisation even if they liked their job and 19% were prepared to actively sabotage the organisation.

FACT: A SURVEY REVEALED THAT 72% OF UK EMPLOYEES DID NOT LIKE THEIR ORGANISATION, EVEN IF THEY LIKED THEIR JOB AND 19% WERE PREPARED TO ACTIVELY SABOTAGE THE ORGANISATION.

Handy proposes an organisation made up of medium to large doughnuts, or group doughnuts – the doughnut principle. The jam in the middle represents what has to be done in any job by an individual or by a group and the ring around the outside is the limit of your authorities. However, in between that space is your area for discretion, your room to make a difference.

In *The Elephant and the Flea*[125], Handy says: "I call this my "doughnut principle", which I believe is the secret to all good work. That is the English doughnut with jam in the middle. The jam represents what has to be done in any job by an individual or by a group and the ring around the outside is the limit of your authorities. But in between that space is your area for discretion, your room to make a difference".

MYTH: Employees need to start on a low salary to gain motivation to get to the top.

Handy also discusses the fact that this inequality has a severe impact in employee retention. According to him, organisations these days are surrounded by many little organisations, often individuals calling themselves an organisation contracted to provide services and advice of one sort of another. "The temptation for the individual frustrated by his/her lack of discretion is to leave the organisation to become a flea riding on the back of the organisation that they were once inside".

"The temptation for the individual frustrated by his/her lack of discretion is to leave the organisation to become a flea riding on the back of the organisation that they were once inside". – Charles Handy

"I call it doing your best with what you are best at; using your talents to the full. Doing your best with what you are best at for the good of others is the secret for a good life. I think that should be the aim of everybody interested in developing other human beings, your children, your workforce or your colleagues. Find out what they are best at and then give them the space to do their best, for the good of others. Actually, to be honest, I think you can apply that to organisations. Doing their best at what they are best at, for the good of others, not just trying to get richer. In the end, that's what organisations can offer; a real chance for everybody to experience Eudemonia and if they can".

In a more comprehensive view, in a paper[126] published by the University of Berkeley, Soosun Tiah You argues that inequality does impede economic and human development, hindering growth through institutions and schooling. Further, he proves that inequality is negatively correlated with all three development measurements: per capita income, institutional performance and secondary school enrolment rate.

MYTH: Some degree of inequality could benefit corporate performance.

This principle also applies within organisations. According to the paper "Performance Pay and Within-Firm Wage Inequality", a report published by the IZA Institute in Norway, it was found that individual performance pay schemes will enhance the effort and output of the most efficient workers and consequently, their pay in order to compensate for effort cost and risk. "As more efficient workers typically have better outside options, the introduction of performance pay also leads to increased wages of workers with high pay in the first place. Thus, when the firm has the power to unilaterally set wages, theory predicts that within-firm wage dispersion is greater with performance pay", the report reads.

However, the report finds that group-based performance pay schemes have minor effects on wage dispersion since effort is more evenly distributed and the risk is pooled across workers. The report concludes that, even though pay for performance is on the rise and does contribute to within-firm wage dispersion, the introduction of performance-based payment schemes is unlikely to be a major contributor to increased wage inequality in the highly unionised European labour markets.

IDEA: To be motivated and commit to their job – thus ensuring a higher level of retention – workers need an appropriate set of incentives, which includes a balanced compensation.

(To comment our ideas, give suggestions and to participate, join our forum at http//www.thesustainableorganisation.com)

OBSERVATION: THE SITUATION COULD BE CHANGING

According to a report by the Hay Group on executive pay, CEO salary and total cash as a multiple of average employee salary and total cash vary significantly across and within sectors. The report states that much of this variance can be explained by the different staffing models across sectors – CEO versus average employees – and individual circumstances in each company. On the whole, the pay multiple seems to reflect variations in average employee pay rather than CEO pay, which reflects the complexity of products/services offered by a company.

Furthermore, the report finds that there is no correlation between pay equality (the CEO-worker ratio) and performance, even within one sector, and suggests that the most pressing call to action for those setting CEO pay is that it reflects the individual circumstances of the company they are leading. In other words, CEO pay needs to match company performance, and not be established individually as the price for that particular CEO. Additionally, it needs to evolve corresponding to a positive evolution in the company itself, which goes against the current situation where we see companies decline, while CEO pay continues to rise.

In fact, data shows that CEO salary and bonus levels do not vary nearly as much as average employee and bonus levels. One explanation could be that CEO salary and bonus actually reflect market capitalisation rather than operational complexity or value at risk. Also, another explanation could be that a focus on market practice and the perceived restrictions put in place by institutional shareholders have created a situation where CEO pay does not reflect individual company circumstances or strategies.

Therefore, with the conclusion that CEO pay does not follow the company's performance as it should, in principle, there seems to be a pressing need to implement this correspondence. It could be concluded that the recent shift in investors' perspectives on pay presents an opportunity for companies and remuneration committees to match CEO pay to individual companies.

"The recent shift in investors' perspectives on pay presents an opportunity for companies to match CEO compensation to the companies' performance"

According to an article published on the Financial Times by Harvard professor Charles W. Elliott, "there is no question that income is distributed substantially more unequally than it was a generation ago, with those at the very top gaining a greater share as even the upper middle class loses ground in relative terms".

While progressives argue that inequality jeopardises the legitimacy of the political and economic system, conservatives defend that the risk is also much higher and that entrepreneurship exerts a key role in advancing economic growth. There is a worry that policy measures taken to combat inequality directly will have adverse effects.

US President Barack Obama recognised this in his Inequality Speech. He believes that America was built on the idea of "broad-based prosperity", giving the example of CEO Henry Ford's decision to pay his workers enough so that they could buy the very cars they built. "Inequality also distorts our democracy", he said. "It gives an outsized voice to the few who can afford high-priced lobbyists and unlimited campaign contributions, and runs the risk of selling of our democracy to the highest bidder", he added. "More fundamentally", he stated further, "this kind of gapping inequality gives lie to the promise at the very heart of America: that is the place where you can make it if you try."

However, there is no doubt that the efforts to fight this inequality are spreading. Nevertheless, Elliott recognises that "inequality is likely to remain high and continue to rise, even in the face of all that can responsibly be done to increase the burden on those with high income and redistribute the proceeds". According to Elliot, the most important step that should be taken to enhance opportunity – the only way more people can be part of those top 1% – "is to strengthen public education".

"The only way more people can be part of those top 1% is to strengthen public education" – Charles W. Elliott

Josh Kraushaar, the political editor for *The National Journal*, agrees with the crucial role of education in the fight against inequality. In an article[127] published in January 2014, he states that US politicians are avoiding the increasing access to quality education, the key in the fight against inequality. He believes that there is a path to closing the gap between poorer children that cannot afford educational opportunities and wealthier ones, but this path is more focused on increasing opportunities than achieving a balanced outcome.

Similarly, a post[128] by Sherry Linkon, former co-director of the Center for Working Class Studies at Youngstown State University and now editor of the blog *Working-Class Perspectives*, argues that elite schools should work harder to recruit working class students and students should continue with their organised protests against cuts to public education. However, Linkon argues that there is more to it than simply focusing on better college education to solve economic inequality. "While a college education still provides economic advantages, increasing lifetime income, achieving that benefit is harder than it used to be. These days, getting a college degree does not guarantee better middle-class job prospects, but it does often bring a lifetime of debt", she argues.

"While a college education still provides economic advantages, increasing lifetime income, achieving that benefit is harder than it used to be". – Sherry Linkon

Although Linkon does not doubt that a good education will bring a great deal of advantages, she argues that only some of these advantages are in fact related with employment or income and education is not enough to address the root causes of the current economic inequality. To resolve this issue, she suggest that public universities prepare students for jobs in specific fields, "like health care or fracking". Secondly, she believes that education does not address the broader economic structure – "moving some people into better paying jobs does not eliminate the low-wage jobs they left behind".

Moreover, Linkon states that we should expect to see more low-wage jobs over time, not fewer "and education won't change that". She concludes: "If we want to improve the lives of low-wage workers and their families, we need public policies that will create more jobs, increase wages and protect people from the financial ravages that often accompany illness, natural disasters and other devastating and expensive events". To this effect, she believes that "activism" and "organisation" are crucial, although these necessarily imply a better education, so that people can "articulate and advocate for their own interests and for the common good".

Global Solution

This chapter presents the different elements that have inspired our proposal for a sustainable organisation.

Firstly, it discusses the way money can successfully impact happiness. Secondly, it introduces the concept of the marginal million to demonstrate that internal motivation can generate economic value.

Then, it describes the crowd organisation, a new structure characterised by the lack of hierarchies and the reinforcement of cooperation. Furthermore, it debates the idea of Super Managers as super heroes or super athletes, in detriment to the average worker.

Finally, it presents a new management model, characterised by the evolution towards a society based on achievement, recognition and motivation.

MONEY IMPACTS HAPPINESS

Daniel Gilbert, a Harvard psychologist, said in his TED Talk entitled *The Surprising Science of Happiness*[129]:

Sir Thomas Brown wrote in 1642: 'I am the happiest man alive. I have that in me that can convert poverty to riches, adversity to prosperity. I am more invulnerable than Achilles; fortune hath not one place to hit me'. What kind of remarkable machinery does this guy have in his head? Human beings have something that we might think of as 'a psychological immune system'. A system of cognitive processes, largely non-conscious cognitive processes, that help them change their views of the world, so that they can feel better about the worlds in which they find themselves. Like Sir Thomas, you have this machine. Unlike Sir Thomas, you seem not to know it.

It may well be that the long-lived cliché "money does not bring happiness" is not – and has never been – entirely true. While some still swear by it, others continue to show the world that having money does not necessarily mean that you lead a happy life. The other side of the coin, however, shows that, if nothing else, having money assures that you surpass obstacles that would otherwise turn your life a bit more complicated, to say the least. This refers to things such as accommodation, food, health and education. In other words, the things you *need* as a basis to lead a happy life.

The well-known hierarchy of needs by Abraham Maslow[130] describes the pattern that human motivations generally move through. It is depicted as a pyramid, with the largest and most crucial levels of needs at the bottom and the need for self-actualisation at the top, although the author himself never used a pyramid to describe these levels of need.

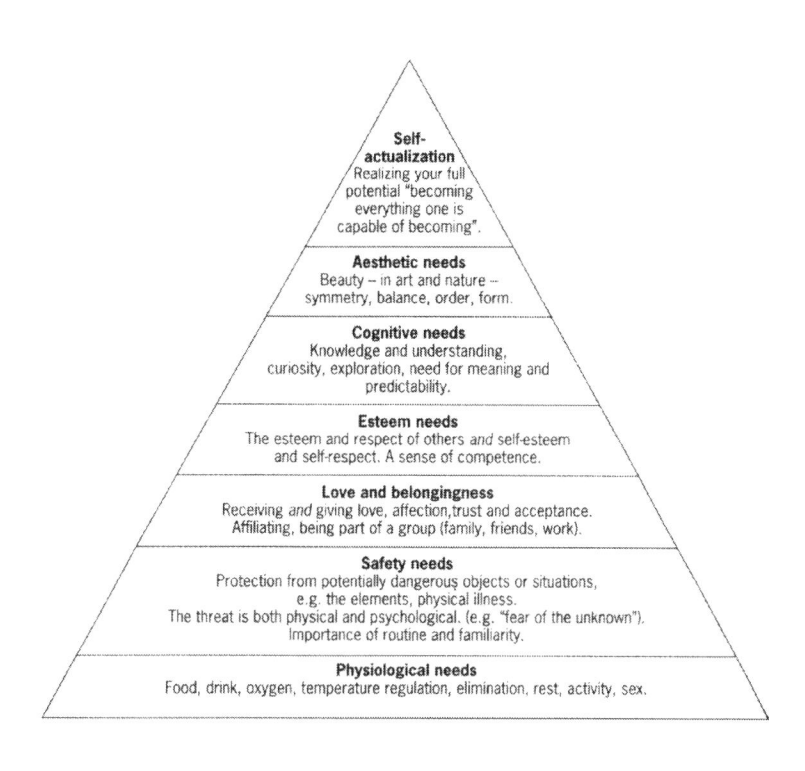

```
                    /\
                   /  \
                  / Self- \
                 / actualization \
                / Realizing your full \
               / potential "becoming \
              /  everything one is    \
             /   capable of becoming". \
            /----------------------------\
           /      Aesthetic needs         \
          /   Beauty – in art and nature –  \
         /   symmetry, balance, order, form. \
        /--------------------------------------\
       /           Cognitive needs              \
      /         Knowledge and understanding,     \
     /      curiosity, exploration, need for meaning and \
    /                  predictability.                \
   /-----------------------------------------------------\
```

Fig. 2 Maslow's hierarchy of needs[131]

According to Maslow, there are four basic and fundamental levels, which he names the "Deficiency Layers". First, Physiological Needs, which include breathing, food, water, sex, sleep, homeostasis and excretion, in other words, the physical requirements for human survival, without which the human body cannot function properly and will fail. For this reason, these should be met before anything else. Secondly, the safety needs, which involve personal, financial and health security and well-being, as well as a safety net against accidents or illnesses and their adverse impacts.

The third level is the interpersonal level of love and a sense of belonging. According to Maslow, friendship, intimacy and family are essential for all humans, to provide them with a sense of belonging and acceptance. The fourth deficiency level is "esteem" and regards the fact that humans have a need to feel respected, which includes self-esteem, self-respect, confidence, achievement, respect of others and respect by others.

Finally, the top level – self-actualisation – refers to the person's full potential, and the realisation of that potential. Maslow describes it as the desire to accomplish everything that one can, to become the most that one can be, and states that, to understand this level of need, the person must not only achieve the previous needs but also master them. Following Maslow's doctrine, to reach our full potential, we need to fulfil needs that involve having a bit of money. In other words, money facilitates the process of reaching our full potential.

Forty years ago, Richard Easterlin took this even further and proposed a paradox entitled "Easterlin Paradox" in a research paper named *Economics of Happiness*[132]. The paradox claims that, within a given country, people with higher incomes are more likely to be happy. However, in international comparisons, he reached the conclusion that the average level of happiness does not vary much with national income per person. Subsequent research also shows that, within a country, more money can mean fewer problems for the poor. In the case of wealthier people, it has been argued that "enough is enough", which is to say, increasing their income by a marginal sum would not necessarily make them happier.

PARADOX: Money never stops buying happiness.

Research by Robert Skidelsky[133], a renowned economic historian, addressed what drives people in affluent societies to seek more money when they know this does not bring them more happiness. While they accept that poor countries need to grow to catch up with western living standards, they wonder why all societies are so obsessed with growth, taking economist John Keynes' assumption that, as consumption reaches certain levels, the incentive to work harder tails off. According to Skidelsky, Keynes' belief did not materialise because 'wants' are relative. Money confers status and many people still live below the poverty line, which means that growth needs to remain a purpose across the world[134].

FACT: MONEY CONFERS STATUS.

A recent Brookings paper by Betsey Stevenson and Justin Wolfers, entitled *Subjective Well-Being and Income: Is there any evidence of satiation?*[135] also analysed this need for wealth, suggesting that, "when it comes to happiness, you can never be too rich". Stevenson and Wolfers believe there is no "satiation point" per se – no amount where happiness does not change, despite an increase in income. Moreover, they have convincing data to prove it: as the rich get richer, the proportion of satisfaction does keep rising, according to the wealthy individuals inquired.

FACT: PEOPLE WITH HIGHER INCOMES ARE MORE LIKELY TO BE HAPPY BECAUSE THEY CAN CATER FOR ALL IMMEDIATE NEEDS.

In their conclusion, they cite the research by Nobel Prize-winning psychologist Daniel Kahneman and Angus Deaton entitled *High income improves evaluation of life but not emotional well-being*[136]. They found that emotional well-being (or "the emotional quality of an individual's everyday experience, the frequency and intensity of experiences of joy, stress, sadness, anger and affection that make one's life pleasant or unpleasant") rises with income, but only to a point. They defined this point as US$75,000 per year. Stevenson and Wolfers do not take issue with this finding, noting that Kahneman and Deaton were looking at different measures and focused only on everyday experiences, while they relied on "affective" questions. "The affective measure raises a puzzle", says Wolfers. "No one has resolved that puzzle. It's an interesting, open question", he says.

PARADOX: Maybe money does buy happiness after all.

In fact, to many, these differences depend on the different measurement scales: whether the population inquired is asked about their general satisfaction, their outlook on life, or the use of the GSS index in market research, which tends to make people think about their lives in a broader context and compare themselves to a wide sector of the humanity. This means that people will always judge their satisfaction comparing their situation to that of others, rather than observing their situation as a whole. In addition, a study by researchers at Stanford and the University of Toronto[137] suggests that money makes people happy and more so for workers paid by the hour than by salary, because this means that people paid by the hour are more often reminded of how much they earn, and this makes money more salient in their thinking.

A different research conducted by Elizabeth Dunn and Michael Norton, co-authors of *Happy Money: The Science of Smarter Spending* and professors at the University of British Columbia and Harvard Business School, demonstrates that, in general, intuitions about how to turn money into happiness are misguided at best and completely wrong at worst. According to them, the things we can actually buy with that money, like TVs, cars and houses have almost no impact on our happiness.

THE THINGS WE CAN ACTUALLY BUY WITH MONEY HAVE ALMOST NO IMPACT ON OUR HAPPINESS (DUNN AND NORTON)

The authors go on to claim that selfless acts do make us happy and, after a series of experiments, they found that asking people to spend money on others, from giving to charity to buying gifts, reliably makes them happier than spending that same money on themselves. Furthermore, their research shows that even in poor countries, individuals who gave to others were happier than those who spent everything on themselves. In one study, they found that asking people to spend as little as US$5 on someone else over the course of a day made them happier at the end of the day than people who spent the US$5 on themselves.

MYTH: Money first, happiness later

We can already observe this in some companies. At Google, for instance, they maintain a fund whereby an employee can nominate another employee to receive a US$150 bonus. This can be seen as a small change, but the nature of the bonus can represent a large emotional payoff, the authors say. The research concludes that by rethinking how we spend our money, we can reap more happiness for every dollar we spend, and by maximising the happiness that employees and customers get from every dollar they receive, companies can increase general satisfaction and benefit the bottom line.

We can conclude that, while people with higher incomes are more likely to be happy, the act of acquiring material things has no impact on happiness and charitable actions actually make people happier than spending money on themselves. In the case of wealthier people, increasing their income by a marginal sum does not necessarily make them happier. However, the bottom line is that, to fulfil the basic needs that enable us to fulfil our potential and pursue a path towards happiness, money comes in as a necessity, which leads us to the conclusion that money is indeed associated with happiness.

PARADOX: Money does not bring or buy happiness

REDISTRIBUTION LEADS TO A BETTER ECONOMIC OUTCOME

"If he has to lose his little finger tomorrow, he would not sleep tonight; but provided never saw them, he would snore with the most profound security over the ruin of a hundred million of his brethren". – Adam Smith, Scottish Philosopher and Economist

Think about any city in the world, the ones with the best quality of living, the ones with the lowest costs, the ones with the most barriers to a higher quality of living, the ones with the steepest prices. Anywhere in the world, if one person earns US$10 million, an extra million would have very little impact in his/her quality of living and happiness. This would seem like a straightforward fact.

It also seems fairly straightforward that, if this extra million (from now on designated 'The Marginal Million') were to be distributed (let's say, among ten people). The ten families would be able to see a palpable improvement in their quality of living with this extra US$100,000, which is considered more than enough for a family to live quite well, in any part of the world!

Although this may seem a naïve interpretation of the subject, in reality, most of the big problems of humankind could be resolved by simple measures – simple, but crucial measures that most complex problems depend upon. In reality, if we focus on looking at how money is created and distributed, we may surely find the source of all major economic problems of societies.

FACT: BIG PROBLEMS CAN BE RESOLVED WITH SIMPLE MEASURES.

Let us take the example of the legendary value investor Warren Buffet, who turned an ailing textile mill into a financial engine that would become the world's most successful holding company. According to Buffett, it is important to focus on the management's competitive advantage in the marketplace, based on the principle of acquiring stock in what he believes are well-managed, undervalued companies. When Buffet makes an acquisition, his intention is to hold the securities indefinitely.

This is the story of one of the world's most successful investors and the turning point is that he has decided he would rather give his money away. This was how he stunned the world in June 2006, when he announced the donation of the vast majority of his wealth to the Bill & Melinda Gates Foundation, which focuses on world health issues, US libraries and global schools.

However, this was nothing new. Warren Buffet has been giving money away for forty years through the Buffett Foundation, renamed as the Susan Thompson Buffet Foundation, which supports pro-choice family planning causes and works to discourage nuclear proliferation. At the time, he explained: "I am not an enthusiast of dynastic wealth, particularly when the alternative is six billion people having that much poorer hands in life than we have, having a chance to benefit from the money".

"I am not an enthusiast of dynastic wealth, particularly when the alternative is six billion people (...) having a chance to benefit from the money" – Warren Buffett.

More recently, in April 2015, Dan Price, the founder of the Seattle-based credit card payment processing firm Gravity Payments, took the bold move to cut his pay after reading the article that inspired the theory of the "Marginal Million"[138]. The article shows that, for people who earn less than US$700,000 a year, extra money makes a big difference in their lives. This has led Price to surprise his staff by announcing that he planned to raise the salary of even the lowest-paid clerk, customer service representative and salesman to a minimum of US$70,000. On top of that, to be able to assure that all employees can reach this amount, Price said he would pay for the wage increases by cutting his own salary from nearly US$1 million to US$70,000 and using 75% to 80% of the company's anticipated US$2.2 million in profit in 2015, the *New York Times* reported[139].

THE MARGINAL MILLION THEORY

This theory is based in a world with annual revenue of between US$50,000 and US$100,000. If this were true among the global population, then we would be able to see a medium class with a high purchasing power. As a result, economies would undoubtedly grow as a whole, the ultimate aim of any country/government. However, the reality is entirely different. What we see is that the current distribution of wealth and revenue is not effective altogether.

According to Princeton University's Daniel Kahneman's study on the price of happiness mentioned above, money can buy happiness, but the line is set at US$75,000. This study, which is solely based on the US population, shows that gaining more than this amount brings no additional happiness. In the UK, for instance, this would mean that a very few have reached this plateau. In fact, according to the Office of National Statistics' annual survey[140], in the tax year ending in April 2012, "the median gross annual earnings for full-time employees on adult rates who had been in the same job for at least 12 months were £26,500" ($43,009), a 1.4% increase compared to the previous year.

Kahneman and his research team concluded: "More money does not necessarily bring more happiness, but less money is associated with emotional pain"[141]. Therefore, the proposal for a sustainable model starts within the company – the entity that is actually producing the wealth. Through an effective corporate governance model, the entity should be able to use that wealth (produced with the help of every single member of staff) and redistribute it accordingly, without any major discrepancies that mean that some may have too much, and others too little. At least that is the general idea…

"More money does not necessarily bring more happiness, but less money is associated with emotional pain" – Daniel Kahneman.

The fact is, this idea sounds both too obvious and too utopic. However, if it seems obvious to everyone – and if redistribution is obviously the way forward to tackle poverty – why has it not been used before? We could name a few factors, like the lack of satisfaction and the lack of consideration for the global situation. What becomes obvious is that there needs to be a change of mentality where we take a "Robin Hood" approach and share our "surplus happiness".

Therefore, with the obvious note that money does help in the path to pursue happiness and using the logic that a severe lack of money strongly contributes to someone's unhappiness, we propose the use of distribution. An extra million, deemed to have very little impact in the improvement of one's quality of living, could be divided among a population that needs more money to attain a comfortable life. Then, this population would be closer to reaching happiness, as they would have access to all basic goods and services.

French economist Thomas Piketty, has also proposed an approach to wealth distribution to curb rising inequality. In *Capital in the Twenty-First Century*[142], he provides an outlook on global inequality heralded to provide a shift in the focus of economic policy towards distribution. Piketty reckons that the importance of wealth in modern economies is approaching levels last seen before the First World War.

As a rule, he explains, wealth grows faster than economic output. Other things being equal, he says, faster economic growth will reduce the importance of wealth in society, whereas slower growth will enhance it. However, he explains, there are no natural forces pushing against the steady concentration of wealth; only a rapid growth caused by technological progress or rising population. Piketty concludes his work by recommending that government step in now and adopt a global tax on wealth to prevent soaring inequality from contributing to economic or political instability.

What we propose is the implementation of the principle that one million in the hands of a few people is worth ten times more, if put in the hands of many. This is based on the concept of redistribution and on the idea that there is such a thing as a "satiation point" which enables the calculation of a marginal amount that can be redistributed among the employees. The result will be a happier community that can use this "marginal" sum to provoke a greater impact in their well-being. Considering that giving money also leads to happiness and satisfaction, this is bound to have a positive impact on both ends.

"Aspiration without opportunity leads to violence". – Nick Hanauer, venture capitalist

FACT: A MEDIUM CLASS WITH A HIGH CAPACITY FOR CONSUMPTION WOULD MAKE ECONOMY GROW.

DOES MONEY BUY EVERYTHING?

The big conclusion here is that, if money buys happiness and if we are happier when we give money to others, redistribution does seem to be the key to general happiness, and the distribution of money can sometimes represent a distribution of happiness.

"The best things in life are free, but impossible to buy!"

IDEA: Create a simple and transparent index to measure the organisation's economic impact in the society

IDEA: Glorify Sustainable Organisations since they benefit all society.

THE CROWD ORGANISATION

"The problem in this world is to avoid concentration of power – we must have a dispersion of power". – Milton Friedman, American Economist

The spread of technology and the increasing speed at which people communicate has also changed the way we interact and the way people organise themselves to work. The concept of "crowd" is used in several processes, from education to business, followed by the need for a community to foster a sense of belonging and thus boost loyalty and integration across the company.

However, the concept of crowdsourcing is fairly recent. It involves the practice of gathering contributions from a large group of people, especially in the online community – a combination of "crowd" and "outsourcing". The word was coined in 2005 by Jeff Howe, a contributing editor at *Wired Magazine* and Mark Robinson, features editor. They observed that businesses were using the Internet to outsource work and concluded at the same time that, "the crucial prerequisite is the use of the open call format and the large network of potential labourers"[143]. The concept now applies to a series of activities, from labour division to voting, funding, finding answers and solutions.

Daren C. Brabham was the first person to define "crowdsourcing" in scientific literature, in an article[144] published in 2008, where he stated: "Crowdsourcing is an online, distributed problem-solving and working model". The idea behind the concept was presented as fairly simple, but highly innovative: a crowd thinks better than one person. So, using the ideas and skills of a crowd can result in higher quality ideas and can enable entrepreneurs that have no access to funding to get investors involved in worthwhile projects that would otherwise not be able to kick off.

A flagrant example of this method is Wikipedia[145], where the company has a crowd with the ability to create their own information, which eventually led to the most comprehensive encyclopaedia in the world (albeit not always being the most reliable source of information). Still, there are plenty of other examples of information sources that resort to the use of a crowd, as well as companies that use crowdsourcing to acquire or receive services. It is now common to hear that a band launched a new album through crowdsourcing, someone published a book through crowdsourcing, or a prototype was created with the help of crowdsourcing.

FACT: A CROWD THINKS BETTER THAN ONE PERSON DOES; USING THE CROWD'S IDEAS OR SKILLS CAN RESULT IN HIGHER QUALITY IDEAS.

Nowadays, there is a wide range of *crowdfunding* websites available, which differ according to purpose and approach, although the concept is usually the same: you post a project to a large group of users – the potential investors – and they fund your project if they are interested in it. They will only charge you when your project has raised some funds, or the full amount needed. The most famous examples include Kickstarter[146], where over US$220 million have been raised for more than 61,000 projects, a great example of how successful the "crowd" method can be. Other examples include Indiegogo[147], Rockethub[148], Gofundme[149] and Razoo[150].

Through this method, it is possible to bypass time-consuming processes like securing financing. The entrepreneur can simply present the idea and the potential investors make a decision assessing this presentation. Also, since there is a huge crowd of investors involved, the contributions are much smaller and thus much easier to obtain.

MOOCs

Along the same line, we have the example of MOOCs (Massive Open Online Courses), which are online courses aimed at unlimited participation and open access via the web. In addition to traditional course materials such as videos, readings and problem sets, MOOCs provide interactivity for the user, and help build a community involving students, professors and teaching assistants. Some examples include Coursera[151], Udacity[152] and edX[153].

MOOCs are a relatively new addition to online and distance learning and only became popular in early 2012, when Daphne Koller and Andrew Ng, both formerly of Stanford University, launched their online learning platform Coursera. The idea behind it is bringing education to the masses, enabling anyone throughout the entire world with access to the Internet to have the opportunity to study college or university level courses, gaining a quality educational experience. All courses are free.

In an article by the Observatory of Borderless Higher Education, Alex Katsomitos argues that these interactive platforms have the potential to create global learning communities as they fully exploit revenue sources like *crowdsourcing* or *crowdfunding*. He goes on to say that, MOOCs can even become platforms for student entrepreneurship. Students develop apps and can create start-ups. However, university leaders and administrators will have to develop new skills for this: they will have to learn how to run a "university-entrepreneur" that can operate as an angel investor and be active in other sectors.

It has been argued that it is difficult to predict the long-term impact of MOOCs because it is a fast-moving target. Its rapid growth demonstrates openness by diverse universities to engage with learners on a new set of terms and with new technologies. This rapid growth indicates the potential pace of change in higher education innovation and the utility of a university's involvement in technology innovation. However, future changes may not be so benign – MOOCs could well expose learners to online distance learning and using innovations that are still not available to all and are not universal either[154].

Although MOOCs have had positive impact on higher education, the idea is not that they should change education on their own. Rather, they are part of a process and should work as a supplement. This is mainly due to the concern that using MOOCs as the sole means of receiving education will result in the lack of social abilities. Nevertheless, they have a revolutionary outcome when it comes to the access to education.

FACT: MOOCS HAVE GIVEN FREE ACCESS TO ONLINE COURSES TO MILLIONS, WITH OVER 6.7 MILLION PEOPLE TAKING AT LEAST ONE ONLINE COURSE.

PEER-TO-PEER

The concept of working as a crowd closely follows the introduction of the "peer-to-peer" concept[155]. Peer-to-peer processes consist on interactions originated from the concept of the P2P distributed computer application architecture, which partitions tasks or workloads between peers. This type of structure turned popular in the 1990s by file sharing systems like Napster and is currently widely used with the concept of torrents.

The concept is inspired in a new type of human interaction and dismisses authoritarian and centralised structures. Although the term was initially coined to apply to computer architecture, it is now widely used on all sectors. This is done under three fundamental aspects: peer production, whereby the production of value is open to participation and use to the widest possible number of users; peer governance, whereby the product is governed by the community, rather than a hierarchy or market; and peer property, whereby services and products are distributed in a non-exclusive manner.

The peer-to-peer structure has been widely implemented across different sectors, but one more recent example is that of a new money transfer system – CurrencyFair.com[156]. This was created in Perth, Australia, by an electrical engineer named Brett Meyers who took the concept to change the way we send money internationally: instead of going through the traditional international banking system, users can use CurrencyFair.com to exchange and send money directly between them.

The system consists of a virtual peer-to-peer foreign exchange marketplace and the result is that the actual cost of sending money internationally is cut by more than 90%. According to Meyers, CurrencyFair was designed to become conducive for saving money whilst sending amounts abroad. It is directed at expats, small and medium businesses, international students, and anyone who needs to take money from one bank account into another one in a different country. It happens quicker than using traditional bank transfers and is 90% cheaper, he said during an interview with Newfination[157].

Meyers gave the example of Irish workers in Perth. Out of those, some are sending euros to Australia and a lot are exchanging Australian dollars into euros. This would mean two international transactions but through CurrencyFair, they only need two domestic transactions. The international affairs attract a large number of fees, but when working together, the situation changes entirely. They only cover 17 countries, but the plan is to cover all countries and get rid of the international swift payment, all over the world. With this, CurrencyFair bypasses the whole system. First, you deposit the money in the client accounts; then, you have a balance with CurrencyFair. Then you can negotiate the exchange and you do not have to worry about transactions because both parties have cleared funds. That speeds up the process and gives us more security.

"Someone has one currency and needs another. Elsewhere, someone else has the second currency and wants the first. CurrencyFair puts the two together over cyberspace". – Jonathan Potter, Co-founder of CurrencyFair

This is more of a marketplace than a bank. Users register and credit their accounts with the money they want to exchange. Then, they look for the best deal that other people on the website are offering and if they see a rate they like, this is "matched" and the sum is transferred from the person's account to the other person's account and vice-versa. The user does not have to match the sum exactly. Rather, he/she simply needs to buy a portion of what is on offer in the market. In fact, the money is never exchanged across borders and as it stays in the country of origin, this results in cuts in bank conversion fees. As a result, users can swap money into euros at close to the pure interbank rate. The only downside of this is that they need to have a bank account in the currency they are swapping into.

FACT: PROCESSES ARE MOVING AWAY FROM CENTRALISATION AND HIERARCHY TO A PEER-TO-PEER STRUCTURE, WHERE EVERYONE HAS EQUAL ACCESS AND THE RIGHT TO PARTICIPATE.

A NEW MONEY MOVEMENT
Along the same lines, there have been several movements to change the way we use money, by changing or bypassing the structures attached to it. The London-based NGO Positive Money[158] is one of these movements and focuses on "the democratisation of money and banking so that it works for society and not against it". The organisation believes that inequality is deeply rooted in money, namely the fact that "the power to create money is mainly in the hands of the same banks that caused the financial crisis". Thus, the organisation states, "taking the power to create money away from banks could give us a more stable economy, more jobs, lower personal debt and affordable housing".

The organisation presents a set of proposals to "fix the design flaw at the heart of the financial system". First, it proposes that "money should only be created through a democratic and transparent body working in the public interest". Therefore, "the power to create money could be transferred to a democratic, accountable and transparent process, where everyone knows who has the power to create money, how much money they create and how that money will be used". Secondly, it proposes, "money should be created free of debt" and then, that "money should come into the real (non-financial) economy before it reaches financial markets and property bubbles. Finally, "banks should not be allowed to create money".

FACT: BANKS CREATE UP TO 97% OF MONEY – IN THE FORM OF THE NUMBERS IN YOUR BANK ACCOUNT – WHEN THEY MAKE LOANS. THIS MEANS THAT THEY EFFECTIVELY DECIDE A) HOW MUCH MONEY THERE IS IN THE ECONOMY AND B) WHERE THAT MONEY GOES. (POSITIVE MONEY)

Other examples of this new vision towards money include Open Money[159], a project to develop a software and infrastructure to enable peer-based multiple local currencies, creating the global infrastructure, tools, governance mechanisms and platforms that will give communities the capacity to create their own currencies "and thereby liberate their wealth potential". "This will become the most important evolution for society in the coming years", the organisation states.

Bitcoin[160] is another well-known example of a decentralised currency, although its impact has been questionable. This is another open source peer-to-peer electronic cash system, with no central server or trusted parties. However, it has become linked to online criminal behaviour as it has the capability of obfuscating online transactions. According to the European Central Bank, this currency system even shares some characteristics with Ponzi schemes[161].

Open Money and Bitcoin follow the concept of P2P currencies, a currency that peers can create or destroy within a network to facilitate interchange between the members of the network. "Additional network dynamics like trust, reputation and quality come into play to regulate the currency by informing peers, in the process of engaging other member peers in the currency system, about the utility of the dealing with a certain peer"[162].

LOCAL CURRENCIES

In line with this cooperative effort, several regions have implemented local currencies[163].

Equal Dollars: Implemented in 1996, in Philadelphia. The currency is earned by doing favours for friends and volunteering. Equal Dollars are accepted at more than 100 local businesses and can be earned through community service, helping people with odd jobs or selling belongings on the exchange's online classifieds database. Most participating businesses accept a combination of Equal Dollars and US dollars and many offer discounts to Equal Dollars users. The executive director of the social service non-profit Resources for Human Development (RHD) that launched the currency, Bob Fishman, explained to CNN: "The US dollar is fine to feed the upper 1%, but we are missing something that gets people to work for each other and for the community… This helps regular people exchange goods and services in an economy that is in deep trouble".

Ithaca Hours: One of the longest-running community currencies in the US, Ithaca Hours, has been used as a model for many other home-grown currencies since 1991. The currency was launched to help stimulate the local economy and now, more than 900 participants currently accept it for goods and services, and several employers issue the currency as part of their wages. The currency was denominated in hours to convey that it is really the time spent helping the community that is being exchanged.

BerkShares: Since 2006, in the small mountain community of Southern Berkshire, Massachussetts, residents can exchange US dollars for this currency and use it at more than 400 local businesses. In order to keep BerkShares in circulation, merchants that try to exchange the currency for US dollars at the bank get charged a 5% fee.

Bay Bucks: In Traverse City, Michigan, a group of residents launched Bay Bucks in 2006, hoping to get more people to spend locally. Bay Bucks are now accepted and circulated by roughly 100 local businesses and a couple of non-profit organisations are paying part of employees' salaries in the currency.

Cascadia Hour Exchange (CHE): In Portland, Oregon, the Cascadia Hour Exchange (CHE) has been up and running since 1993. The currency facilitates bartering among locals and was modelled after Ithaca Hours. With CHEs, members can negotiate prices for goods and services with other people or businesses that accept them.

Life Dollars: In Belligham and Seattle, Washington, Life Dollars[164] were created in 2004 to replace US dollars altogether, according to Francis Ayley, who founded the currency. Membership increased to the point that the currency spread to Seattle. Almost all of the transactions occur online: members have online accounts where they can transfer money directly to other members and businesses.

Downtown Dollars: In Ardmore, Philadelphia, John Durso, who heads a non-profit business association called the Ardmore Initiative, formed a local currency called "Downtown Dollars" in 2010. Each community member was able to go to the Initiative and exchange $100 of their own money for 200 Downtown Dollars, which retailers would accept as $200 US dollars, essentially providing customers with a 50% discount. The store owner could then simply take the Downtown Dollars to the Initiative and exchange them for $200 US dollars.

Local Trade: In Faytetteville, Arkansas, Local Trade Partners was founded in 2009 as a hybrid between a local currency and old-fashioned bartering, letting local businesses exchange services for "trade dollars". An auto repair man can change the oil in someone's car, for example, and that person can pay him in trade dollars. The repairman can then use that money at the local restaurant or even at the dentist. Because the aim is to help local businesses, members must be business owners and they are required to live locally.

Crescents: In New Orleans, the rise of the debit card use spurred one farmers market to make its own money. In 2004, a growing number of shoppers wanted to put their purchases on plastic, but the local farmers didn't have the machines to accept the card, so the market's coordinators stepped in and created Crescents. Customers can buy the wooden coins with checks, debit cards or food stamp benefit cards when they arrive at the market and then shop at the stands. Vendors who get paid in the coins can use them somewhere else that accepts them, maybe another vendor in the market.

Outside the US, this phenomenon is also spreading. In England, the **Lewes Pound** was launched in 2008 as a five-year pilot project of Transition Lewes. Similarly, the **Totnes Pound**, the **Bristol Pound** and the **Brixton Pound** were implemented across the country. Canada already counts on the use of **Calgary Dollars, Toronto Dollars** and **Salt Spring Dollars**, while Japan already has a time bank called **Fureai Kippy**, where you can earn credits by helping the elderly, among other tasks.

THE FULL CROWDSOURCING ORGANISATION

This proposal entails a decentralisation where a peer-to-peer structure can be implemented to create "a full crowdsourcing organisation", where management is based on the "crowd" prefix, and not centralised or subject to strict hierarchies. That is to say, a management founded on 'crowdthinking', 'crowdteaming', 'crowdfunding', 'crowdstaffing' and 'crowdselling'.

These are the concepts behind each step of the company's administration, under the principle that, the wider the group of contributors, the better the result. Through the efforts of a crowd, companies can achieve better results, directed at the welfare of participants rather than to the interest of a few.

FACT: THROUGH THE EFFORTS OF A CROWD, A COMPANY CAN ACHIEVE BETTER RESULTS.

Therefore, by allying this sense of community and cooperation with tools such as rewards in compliance with a median, the longevity of the company, community size and innovation – always avoiding and penalising speculation – the company can stick to its real mission: creating something useful to benefit its customers. This creates a cooperative effort to stay at the top, which will necessarily bring with it recognition, replacing the concept of 'wage' by that of 'reward'.

Thus, organisations can turn into cooperatives – crowd organisations. Here, good leaders willing to integrate this change movement will turn into agents of effective change, thus assigning the company a role in terms of revenue distribution within the society and turning companies into a more significant agent than the State. The State, in its turn, would see the mass of taxpayers increase, as they step out of wage slavery to become effective contributors to economic growth.

Here, we could say that the only ones who suffer a negative impact, in principle, would be the leaders. However, considering the theory of the marginal million, and the measurement of happiness, one could argue that, if they gain respect, influence and work, they are in fact gaining from this change. While good leaders will face this as a challenge, bad leaders will see it as a threat to their status quo.

THE PROBLEM WITH SUPER MANAGERS

"Your most precious possession is not your financial assets. Your most precious possession is the people you have working there, and what they carry around in their heads, and their ability to work together." – Robert Reich, American political economist

Some leaders, the so-called Super Managers, are widely admired for skills that should be part of strategy and leadership. However, the problem arises when confidence balloons into the belief that a Super Manager can win in any situation, because they tend to refuse to accept that some forces are beyond their control and underestimate limitations on opportunities, says Cynthia Montgomery, in *The Strategist: Be the Leader Your Business Needs*[165].

We believe that this idea that Super Managers being like Super Athletes needs to be clarified. The current reality is that Super Managers tend to work in cartel or monopoly industries chosen by political criteria, rather than potential for value creation and distinguished by the value they generate. This results in a reduction of the level of competitiveness of the market, with the aim to eliminate competition.

Alan Kaplan argued that we see CEOs and senior management as the "stars" of the business world, comparable to professional athletes in terms of the impact they have on their organisations and the conflicts of interest that they face. His analysis shows that, while both groups are paid similar amounts, CEOs and senior management are paid mainly in stock options and other forms of variable compensation, while professional star athletes are paid almost exclusively through a fixed salary. We propose turning these "Super Managers" into actors in a collaborative or crowd-based company, which is bound to make organisations more efficient.

JACK WELSH

Jack Welsh is at the forefront of the Super Managers who became increasingly concerned with the concept of "change management" – an approach to transitioning individuals, teams and organisations to a desired future state. This approach was first implemented by McKinsey consultant Julien Phillips, in 1982, with the publication of a change management model, although it took around a decade for peers to catch up. This organisational change consists on a structured approach in an organisation to ensure that changes are smoothly and successfully implemented to achieve lasting benefits. It affects all departments of an organisation and entails strategies, the measurement system, as well as implementation and organisational change.

The General Electric chairman declared war against the managers who resisted the new people-based values arguing that they "get their results without regard to values, and in fact often diminish them by grinding people down, squeezing them, stifling them". His reaction was to dismiss these managers by using the autocratic power of dismissal to inculcate democracy, arguing that "it had to be done if we wanted GE people to be open, to speak up, to share".

Welsh also wanted people to "act boldly" outside "traditional lines of authority" and "functional boxes" in this new "learning, sharing environment". His argument was that short-term thinking damages the long-term interests of a company, not only by the actions it encourages, but also because it undermines people-based management. People who are expected to respond only to orders will eventually act accordingly, he explained.

"Managers get their results without regard to values, and in fact often diminish them by grinding people down, squeezing them, stifling them" – Jack Welsh

IDEA: CEOs should be measured by the value they create into the community, the shareholders and the members of the company.

OTHER INNOVATORS

Steve Jobs is an obvious name when talking about CEOs that left a mark in the industry. In fact, he was known for having completely changed the landscape of the computer industry through Apple and it is undeniable that he revolutionised the way that everyday people think about computers and how they fit in our lives. His concept was that everyone should own a computer, and that these should be easy to use. He used this premise to lead the manufacturing of computers built for the masses.

What seems to be truly remarkable is that Jobs brought the company to greatness right from the beginning, the Famous CEOs list states. Steve Jobs and Steve Wozniak launched the company with the aim of creating what Jobs came to call "insanely great technology". With the development of competition, Apple decided to cling to its original purpose and was nearly bankrupt. It was only when Steve Jobs returned and reinvented the firm in a host of new industries that the company rose to the top again.

Bill Gates also comes at the top of the list as one of the most prominent CEOs of all times. After having revolutionised the industry, he came to become one of the richest people in the world, and now devotes his time to the Bill & Melinda Gates Foundation, which has benefited from billions of dollars from the legacy of Warren Buffett. Like Jobs, Gates led the creation of products to the masses that were extremely user-friendly.

However, his success did not just come from being at the right place at the right time – he also had the acumen to seize the right opportunities, eventually changing the way we work each day, and how we perceive the ownership of computer applications.

In *From Strategy Rules*, by David B. Yoffie and Michael A. Cusumano, Bill Gates, as well as Steve Jobs and Intel's Andy Grove had specific traits that turned them into outstanding CEOs[166]. "They got into the trenches with their employees in the areas where they believed they could add the most value, but always remained focused on the big picture – their higher-level strategic goals or product ambitions. (…) In other words, they didn't just "follow the money". They followed the knowledge". According to Gates, the human factor is key in this process. "It doesn't matter if you have a perfect product, production plan and marketing pitch; you'll still need the right people to lead and implement those plans. That is a lesson you learn quickly in business".

The CEO of Brazilian Semco, Ricardo Semler, has been described as the best low-profile CEO in business today. He does not make decisions because these are made where they will be lived out and it is the stakeholders throughout the company who are responsible for Semco entering a variety of industries and growing dramatically year after year. As a "Participation Age Leader"[167] he believes he is free to ask questions, cast visions and work with others to build the future of Semco, instead of making decisions others can make.

Therefore, Semler has trained others to make decisions, in contrast to the so-called "supermanagers" who are well known for not delegating and getting few hours of sleep per night, making themselves indispensable – which gives them zero points from the point of view of sustainability. At Semco, Semler has six co-CEOs who rotate leadership every six months, allowing the CEO to function at the highest levels of leadership and not make decisions. This has made him fully dispensable, in contrast to Super Managers.

It is evident that this approach has borne fruit. Semco gets hundreds of applications and nobody ever wants to resign. Even in the worst 10-year recession in the history of Brazil, revenues have grown by 600% and profits were up by 500% while productivity rose by 700%.

Frederick W. Smith at FedEx is another top CEO of all times. When he took the money left for him by his passing father in 1971 and started Federal Express, he recognised a need in the marketplace and went for it. Through the years, FedEx faced stiff competition through an improved postal service, other courier companies and modern day technology, but they prevailed, partly due to Smith's quick reactions to trends in the marketplace. For example, when things went rough, he reduced his own salary, as well as those of many executives and top managers to protect the business. Since then, he has managed to sustain considerable growth when the idea became obsolete, growing his company in a way that others believed would not 'fly'.

Other commonly mentioned stories of super management include Starbuck's revolution in the coffee hour business and IKEA's high profits in the furniture industry, both of them strategies that came from a deep comprehension of the industries involved, by the minds of Super Managers. These leaders developed strategies that overcame industry forces by adding new value to old games, and this was only possible because they had a clear sense of their business's added value in those contexts.

When saying that there is a problem with Super Managers, what we mean is that, for people to consider them as Super Managers, these executives need to stand out in a way that their name becomes the image of their company's performance. It is a fact that people-based values are becoming increasingly important in a world where these Super Managers still rule without any regard for the people they work with. In the words of Jack Welsh, "people need to be open, to speak up, to share".

Although it is not always true that the "super" performance of a manager is always linked to his/her performance, this comes to show that their recognition is necessarily tied to a good performance. However, we still believe that it is essential to link this performance to the collaboration with the team, discussed in the chapter entitled "The Crowd Organisation". Leaders should lead by example and motivate others to follow their actions.

IDEA: Investigate the real economic impact of the world top 100 corporations

A NEW MANAGEMENT MODEL

As mentioned previously in this chapter, short-term thinking is founded on the misguided idea that money buys respect. This principle has given rise to the need to create a recognition system based on values and respect, instead of power, greed and competitiveness – an evolution from a society based on power that is imposed, to power that is conquered and based on the respect and recognition, which comes from conquering that power. These premises are based on the belief that money by itself is not fulfilling to someone who is already a millionaire, and thus money cannot be the sole motivation.

To move from this short-term thinking to a more sustainable and long-term arrangement – from a profit-oriented model to an economy-oriented model – we believe that there should be a set of replacements, which we will describe further in our proposal. We believe that these replacements make it possible to have a company that is evaluated according to its full economic value rather than its stock market capitalisation.

This concept of full economic value means that the products sold by the company, or the services it provides, will have an impact in the market where it operates and the communities it touches, through the value of its products or services perceived by the market as well as the economic value of its internal community. In other words, the company sees its value measured by its actual object of valuation – products or services – and by the impact those have in the general community it serves.

This concept distances our society from the concept of wage slavery[168], whereby a person's livelihood depends on wages, especially when this dependency is total and immediate. Rather than a means of survival, wages become a compensation for a joint effort through a concerted goal, in accordance to the employee's contribution and not the value decided by a biased market controlled and dominated by big players.

In sum, if we play rather than compete, there will always be a positive outcome. Similarly, if an organisation operates towards a common goal, it will tend to generate an economic value that is much higher than when it merely competes with other organisations. Moreover, the total human value generated will be incomparable. This is also tied to the principles of power, envy and competition – which we believe undermine sustainability – as they unfortunately lead to a sense of insecurity, inequality, and even, hate. With the implementation of cooperation, we believe these can change to a greater sense of job security and equality among the members of the community as well as the resulting sense of enjoyment that comes from cooperating towards a common goal.

FACT: IN GAME THEORY, IF ONE PLAYS RATHER THAN COMPETES, THERE WILL ALWAYS BE A POSITIVE OUTCOME.

Therefore, moving towards long-term thinking brings the need to link top management to an image of respect and recognition, which is bound to result in more security – at work, in life – opportunities to cooperate, to engage in different activities, to show their worth and harmony. Ultimately, the compensation and profits will pass on this image of recognition, allied to motivation and respect, the ultimate reward.

To this effect, CEOs need to understand that employee compensation is not simply another business cost and indirect costs such as training productivity and opportunity costs can represent the real expense of employee absence. It is evident that the recession has profoundly affected all aspects of the economy and that employers are looking for better ways to attract and retain the right talent. However, the effects of this recession, together with the emergence of a multicultural and multigenerational workforce, as well as the influence of globalisation, have helped focus on innovative employers and their way of keeping their employees happy and productive, despite the economic forces around them.

IDEA: Adapt and adopt the peer-to-peer and open source models to wider implementation in organisations

PUTTING PEOPLE FIRST

When it comes to people-based values, the SAS Institute continues to be an example to follow, particularly due to its personal employee benefits, while Google comes as an example in terms of best practices in employee retention and happiness. Both companies have tapped into new ways of motivating employees – the so-called 'employee enrichment', a strategic concept that focuses on the quality of people's lives and addresses work and non-work life factors to enhance people's lives under the expectation that, the better the person's well-being, the better the person's performance.

This concept of 'employee enrichment'[169] also entails the provision for an employee's professional development through policies aimed at advancing the employee's career and progress. An example of this is the Future Leaders Apprentice programme at Deloitte[170], one of the "big four" professional financial services firms, whereby employees are nominated or selected by committee and all new hires are immediately eligible. The programme offers several weeks of apprentice work at various organisations or departments across the company and in the end, over three-fourths of the employees who take part acquire a higher level position in the firm.

These programmes enable employees to gain a broader vision of the organisation, to feel part of the project and ultimately, to find out whether or not they identify themselves with the organisational culture. This idea is clearly based on a people-first approach, rather than the practices themselves. Similarly, companies like Google, Microsoft, Wells Fargo, SAS, Andrade Gutierrez and Cisco have implemented equivalent measures, and are frequently praised for their treatment of employees. The result is a level of loyalty and passion, which indicates that these methods have a tremendously positive impact on employees and the organisation.

FACT: EMPLOYEE ENRICHMENT HAS RESULTED IN EMPLOYEE LOYALTY AND PASSION.

SAS INSTITUTE

The SAS Institute – the flagship of this new management model – was ranked first on Great Place to Work®'s Top 25 multinational workplaces study[171], due to its uncommon philosophies, methods and intentions and their premise that feelings and emotions are the true drivers of employee loyalty, innovation and productivity, and purposely have made workforce happiness one of their primary missions.

A report by Fast Company on the success of SAS states: "SAS has found that by being an especially benevolent and respectful organisation, they consistently produce the most optimal workplace performance. Their instinct is that workers instinctively and positively respond to an organisation that routinely demonstrates that they matter and are individually valued".

"Feelings and emotions are the true drivers of employee loyalty, innovation and productivity", SAS Institute

Fast Company identified a set of unique values that make SAS stand out. First of all, the fact that it values people above all else, which was obvious at the onset of the 2008 recession, when the software industry was hit by a reduction in spending. At the time, several of SAS' competitors announced massive layoffs, but SAS Institute's CEO Jim Goodnight announced that none of the 130,000 employees would lose their jobs. He took this decision based on the conviction that "what makes this organisation work is the new ideas that come out of his employees' brains", and holds them all in the highest esteem. By putting his employees at peace, he was sure they would produce breakthrough products while his competitors were cutting costs.

What makes this organisation work are the new ideas that come out of the employees' brains – Jim Goodnight.

Secondly, SAS bases its actions on the principle that, "to give, is to get". This is proven by the benefits the company gives to employees and their families: free access to a gym, fully-staffed on-site, healthcare clinic, deeply discounted childcare, "work-life counselling" and common work areas routinely filled with snacks and treats. Goodnight believes that benefits are symbolic representations of how he and his company value its people, and that the way employees are treated will have an impact on their loyalty and engagement. This has been proven by the company's annual turnover rate – 2% to 3% – compared to the industry average of 22%.

Thirdly, SAS believes in "trust above all things". To the CEO, the foundation of the employee happiness at SAS is its culture of trust. By ensuring that workers respect the organisation's management, he knows they will be committed and will contribute. Therefore, the company measures work sentiment and engages the Great Place to Work Institute to independently evaluate the standing of its leadership team. One of the measures it takes to earn trust, is giving employees a lot of freedom on the hours they work and when they use any of the campus services.

CMO Jim Davis told Fast Company: "While we say we have a 35-hour workweek, I don't know anybody who really works 35 hours. The reality is if you trust people, and you ask them to do something--and you treat them like a human being as opposed to a commodity where you try to squeeze something out – they are going to work all sorts of hours. But they're going to enjoy those hours as opposed to 'slaving in the office.'"

"If you trust people and ask them to do something – and you treat them like a human being as opposed to a commodity where you try to squeeze something out – they are going to work all sorts of hours" – Jim Davis.

Finally, SAS Institute makes sure that employees understand the significance of their work. The organisation goes to great lengths to ensure that employees understand how they make a difference. For instance, programmers get to own the work they produce for as long as they work for the firm. Knowing that they will use what they create for a decade or more, inspires them to fully invest in the quality of everything they do, Goodnight explains. Similarly, landscapers employed by the firm are given dedicated acreage to care for so they come to treat it as their own.

Through this innovative leadership model, SAS Institute believes – and this has proven to be true – that employees are happier, more engaged and produce exceptional work. Thus, "customers are more loyal because products have fewer bugs and their contacts at the firm rarely change".

However, one of the main differences between SAS and most other Fortune 500 firms is that SAS is privately held and is thus not influenced by the short-term objectives of shareholders. Nevertheless, the fact that the company has proven the effects of this leadership model that rewards all constituents, creating happier, more engaged employees who produce exceptional work, can be used as an example to other organisations.

GOOGLE'S SUCCESS

Google is another constant presence on ranking for best places to work. The incomparable benefits given to employees seem to match the company's efforts into devoting the same level of intellectual firepower to discover, refine and implement leadership practices that optimise human performance in the workplace. In contrary to widespread practices, Google reveres its employees and seeks to appeal to their minds in motivating performance.

According to the report by Fast Company, Google also owes this to a distinct set of practices. Firstly, the fact that being a great place to work is at the firm's DNA. In fact, the founders – Larry Page and Sergey Brin – used SAS Institute as the company worth emulating. At the time, they met personally with SAS executives and sent a team of people to their headquarters. Collectively, they validated their understanding that people truly thrive in their jobs and remain loyal to them when they feel supported and valued.

FACT: PEOPLE TRULY THRIVE IN THEIR JOBS AND REMAIN LOYAL TO THEM WHEN THEY FEEL SUPPORTED AND VALUED (GOOGLE).

This principle led to the launch of several benefits and a culture based on trust, transparency and inclusion. With this in mind, the firm tried to ensure its own sustainable success, rather than gain a competitive advantage.

Secondly, Google ensures that people have an inspiring job. For years, the company has given every employee the opportunity to devote up to 20% of their workweek to a project of their choice. Typically, Googlers choose to help some other company venture, although this is up to each employee and does not depend on job titles or pay levels.

Thirdly, employees at Google have an uncommon freedom and control of their time. Employees have a greater discretion on work hours and leisure activities, but the firm purposely selects ambitious people with proven records of accomplishment. "That means we are harnessing energy rather than coaxing it out of people", says Prasad Setty, VP of people analytics and compensation. The result has been that employees routinely exceed management's expectations.

Finally, Google is a democracy and employees have a significant voice. The company shows uncommonly aspirational ambitions that employees find motivating and inspiring, but the main driver is that the firm believes that it is truly important to give people a real influence in how the firm is run. One of the measures it takes to implement this is requesting employee feedback on everything they do and giving employees access to company information.

"It is truly important to give people a real influence in how the firm is run" – Google

This new management model has shown to be effective by the tremendous success of companies like Google and the SAS Institute. They have truly created the concept of "dream job". If employees are the ones that really make the company, then it becomes evident that implementing a set of principles and values focused on the employees will bring the company positive results.

Although some argue that these rankings are based on applications by the companies, Glassdoor annually discloses the Employees' Choice Awards, which lists the 50 best places to work, relying solely on the input of employees who anonymously provide feedback through a survey. The survey asks employees to rate their satisfaction with the company's overall and key workplace factors, such as career opportunities, compensation and benefits, work-life balance, senior management, culture and values.

In one of these lists, Facebook was ranked as the top employer for the second time, with an overall ranking of 4.7 out of 5. According to the employees' feedback, the company offers great perks and benefits to help them balance their work with their personal lives, like paid vacation days, free food and transportation, US$4,000 in cash for new parents, dry cleaning, day care reimbursement and photo processing. Nevertheless, they also praise the opportunity to impact a billion people, the company's commitment to its hacker culture and trust in their CEO Mark Zuckerberg.

Global management consulting firm McKinsey & Co. comes second, with 4.5. According to Glassdoor, employees often comment on the impact they have on organisations worldwide, the opportunity to connect with top executives and the access to a valuable network of global colleagues. Finally, rounding out the top three with 4.5 is the San-Francisco based technology company Riverbed, frequently praised as "an exciting and fast growing company where senior leaders are committed to transparency" and a place "with fun events that support family involvement". It seems obvious that employees seem to value their work-life balance and the sense of purpose they get, as well as the opportunity to have an impact.

(If you have other interesting cases, please share it at:
http//www.thesustainableorganisation.com)

Our Global Solution

Following these premises, our global solution is based on the principle that, to the poorer, money is important for happiness; to the richer, there is a satiation point where selfless acts prove more crucial to attaining this happiness. This means that one solution would be to focus on the redistribution to lead to a better economic outcome, and more happiness – our "Marginal Million Theory".

Secondly, there is a widespread recognition of the power of managers, which has led to an image that associates them with super athletes, although this is not necessarily based on skills, but rather on their economic return or the stock performance of the organisation. Here, in line with our long-term goal of widespread sustainability, it becomes essential that managers follow the examples of our inspirational strategists and acquire people-based values: working with everyone towards a goal that everyone shares among them.

Thirdly, in line with the aim of attaining a higher cooperation within the community, crowdsourcing comes as a good example of what can be achieved when we focus on this cooperation. Crowdfunding, MOOCs, peer-to-peer infrastructures and new money movements are essential elements to create a Full Crowdsourcing Organisation, where the different levels are inter-dependable and follow a 'neural' order, aiming to achieve the very same goal.

Finally, joining the aforementioned premises enables the creation of a new management model, focused on achieving socio-aggregated economic value by putting people first and creating an outcome that can be shared among all participants – the community.

IDEA: Create a ranking of the most useful organisations in the world

PART II

In this part of the book, we present our proposal for a model that can boost sustainability in any organisation.

This is not a compilation of facts and it does not have to be read randomly; it follows a methodology where a proposal is illustrated with questions and quotes to inspire the reader to think about the subject under discussion.

THE SUSTAINABLE ORGANISATION MODEL

The aim of our proposal is to suggest tools that can turn organisations sustainable, that is to say, able to maintain their activities in the long-term without a significant deterioration of human well-being and productive capacity, through a process that involves a set of new values and practices.

We take on a series of analogies that compare the current management system (the Old Economy) with a military system, where leaders are at the top of a well-defined hierarchy and coordination structured by relations of power – a system that has become widespread since its use in the Roman Army.

We propose a move from this heavily military structure to a structure characterised by cooperation, using the analogy of an orchestra, where the conductor works in coordination with the musicians towards a common goal and recognition is widespread among all the members of the orchestra.

Then, we take on the analogy of mercenaries and missionaries to illustrate the leaders of the Old Economy and the New Economy, respectively. We propose a shift from management models based on authority to models based on recognition, taking the example of "missionary" CEOs who have chosen to abolish titles and empower their employees, instilling a sense of transparency and true merit to implement the consequent recognition.

Thirdly, we discuss the shift from unfair wages to a fair reward, whereby sustainable organisations no longer relate to wage slavery and adopt practices based on the premises of transparency, merit, accountability, balance and common sense to reach a much-desirable harmony that will enable the members of the organisation to reach their ultimate goal: happiness.

Finally, we dive into the concept of volatility that so greatly describes the current focus on the importance of stock market value. We take on the view that sustainable organisations should not be characterised by a focus on such volatile

ELEMENTS AND SHOULD INSTEAD BE CONCENTRATED ON ACTUAL VALUE CREATION OVER TIME.

"Change is the law of life. And those who look only to the past or present are certain to miss the future." — John F. Kennedy

The following diagram illustrates a syntheses of our model: At the left, the 4 pillars that characterise the Old Economy organisation model; in the middle, the 16 drivers of change towards sustainability; and at the right the 4 pillars that characterise a Sustainable Organisation – rooted in cooperation, meritocracy and fair rewarding to attain full sustainability.

To instil the evolution or revolution, depending on the organisation – from a typical organisation to a sustainable organisation – these 16 drivers are the essential tools of change.

SUSTAINABLE ORGANISATION

Old Economy	Drivers	Sustainable Organisation
Competition	• Trust • Versatility & Flexibility • Empowerment, Mentoring • Passion, Optimism	**VALUES** **Cooperation**
Authority	• Transparency • Knowledge & Influence • Respect • Commitment	**RELATIONSHIPS** **Recognition**
Unfair wages	• Adequate metrics & Accountability • Harmony • Full Mobilization • Meritocracy	**METRICS** **Fair Rewarding**
Shareholder's Value	• Internal & External Impact • Usefulness, Meaning • Non-speculative • Sustainability	**PURPOSE, GOALS** **SUSTAINABLE ORGANISATION**

Fig. 3 – The Sustainable Organisation model

In the following pages, we will describe in detail how to implement this evolution.

1 – FROM COMPETITIVENESS TO COOPERATION

"The most important single central fact about a free market is that no exchange takes place unless both parties benefit." – Milton Friedman, American economist, Nobel Laureate in Economics, on an interview to PBS

"The economic services that it [the division of labour] can render are insignificant compared with the moral effect that it produces, and its true function is to create between two or more people a feeling of solidarity." – Emile Durkhein, French sociologist and philosopher, in "The Division of Labour in Society"

"Even in the angels there is the subordination of one hierarchy to another, and in the heavens, and all the bodies that are moved, the lowest by the highest and the highest in their turn unto the Supreme Mover of all." – Saint Ignatius, Patron Saint of Soldiers

"In most companies, the formal hierarchy is a matter of public record – it's easy to discover who is in charge of what. By contrast, natural leaders don't appear on any organisation chart." – Gary Hamel, American management expert

"In a hierarchy, every employee tends to rise to his level of incompetence." – Laurence J. Peter, Canadian educator and "hierarchiologist"

"I think it only makes sense to seek out and identify structures of authority, hierarchy, and domination in every aspect of life, and to challenge them; unless a justification for them can be given, they are illegitimate, and should be dismantled, to increase the scope of human freedom." – Noam Chomsky

"To work without love is slavery". – Mother Teresa

A WORLD OF HIERARCHIES

Twelve-year-old J. is a highly-aspiring member of the Mormon Church and knows that, to advance through the levels of priesthood and become a senior apostle – or even the President of the Church – he will have to compete with the 15 million members and go through the small church units (Wards). He knows that, in addition to that, he has to reach the wider church units (Stakes) and integrate the First and Second Quorum of the Seventy, the group of full-time Church workers split into area presidencies. From here, he can only hope to integrate the highly exclusive Quorum of the Twelve Apostles, the only level below the President of the Church and his two counsellors. If J. were to be born a woman, her chances would have changed entirely: the only leadership position she could have would be as an auxiliary associated with women and children and she would not be allowed to hold Priesthood.

In Tibet, fully-devoted Buddhist J., would also face a long ladder of levels to integrate a Buddhist monastery and become a monk – the highest position in the Buddhist religious hierarchy. He would leave behind Buddhist nuns, lay people and pilgrims, although this stratification would be slightly different from that of the Mormon Church. In Buddhist terms, hierarchy is a sort of etiquette: who should show respect to whom, who should bow down to whom. As a monk, everyone would have to bow down to him and if J. were a novice nun – the lowest of ordained women – even kings would bow down to her. This stratification is at the very heart of Tibetan Buddhism[172] as a form of scholasticism: a global view that revels in creating divisions, distinctions and organising them in clear schemes. Even amongst monks, J. would find different types of treatment that depend on the level and time of ordination.

In the Old Continent's Catholic Church, J. would also face a great deal of steps to get to the ultimate level of Christianity – the Pope. Below, the structure includes Cardinals, Archbishops, Bishops, who control the diocese and the cathedrals, Priests who control parishes and the Catholics themselves in the bottom of the structure. If J. decided to devote fully to the Catholic Church, he would have to lead the faithful at local and increasingly higher levels. He would start by the parish (the most basic level), followed by the diocese, the archdiocese, and then the Church – the highest point being the Pope who oversees the Church and its faithful from his home in the Vatican City[173].

Maybe it is not a coincidence that, even in heaven, under the perspective of the Bible, there is a hierarchy. After all, what better way to impose the "benefits" of accepting the power of a hierarchy in the human mind? Whatever the religion, we are formatted to accept hierarchy without any questions and while most management studies discuss business models, organisation and power structure, they seldom question the different types of hierarchies. One has to wonder if this hierarchy really is an absolute truth…

Now, if J. decided that what he wanted was to devote to his motherland, he could join the military. Here, armed forced, police and intelligence agencies wear uniforms or insignia to denote someone's particular rank, in what is a highly complex system codified in the Geneva Convention. Officers, non-commissioned officers, warrant officers and enlisted personnel are only some of the ranks, which present several subdivisions. In the US Army, for instance, J. could obtain 29 different insignia depending on the Army rank obtained.

In theory, it would be up to J. to enter these complex systems of stratification. However, if J. had been born in India, he could integrate a complex system of social class division at birth, where some people would be considered superior and others inferior in an innate condition. Here, J. could be lucky enough to be born within the Brahmins, the most respected and prestigious people, engaged in attaining the highest spiritual knowledge, or even the Kshatriyas or Rajputs (the king and the people who belonged to royal families, the governing body of the society, enjoying special rights and powers). His life would have been entirely different if he was born among Vaisyas, the ones who performed the productive labour, pastoral tasks, trade and agriculture, or among the Shudras, the lowest class of this social hierarchy, who worked as servants to the three other classes and had little or no rights or power of their own.

"In the long run, a hierarchical society was only possible on a basis of poverty and ignorance." – George Orwell

DEFYING HIERARCHIES

In terms of organisational models and human relationship models, humankind has not evolved much over the last millennia. In fact, most organisations still heavily rely on strong hierarchical models, where power, greed and internal competition are the main driving forces. Even non-governmental organisations fit this hierarchical structure, with their board of directors, which supervises the director(s), who in turn supervise the different layers of managers, who supervise the workers at the bottom of the pyramid.

While religious organisations represent a good example of top-down hierarchical systems and the military is organised with a never-ending system of ranks almost streamlined across the world, even society itself still denotes some use of a class-based system. Wherever used, this hierarchical structure always represents a vision of power and victory.

DO WE NEED HIERARCHY?

It is our belief that these relations of power and strong hierarchies, which have been brought by the need to compete, are highly damaging for the sustainability of organisations. This is because they lead to the creation of faulty structures, like monopolies and cartels, and make the functioning of organisations individual and passive: employees struggle and aim to achieve a higher rank and tend to receive little recognition for their contribution.

Along Doerr's previsions mentioned later in this chapter, we believe it is time to evolve and adapt existing organisational models to the new technology, culture and knowledge of the 21st century. This can be done through the evolution from a model that is purely based on power and victory to a model based on Cooperation – a structure we will from now on describe as "neural".

This "neural" structure is distant from vertical structures, but it is not simply a horizontal structure, nor is it a circular structure. To understand the concept of "neural" hierarchy, we will take the example of the human brain, most specifically brain cells. These are characterised by a series of links that are interdependent and that only function properly when the whole system is operating efficiently. A failure at one point will necessarily have an impact on the remaining points of the system and may be compensated by them.

In fact, the brain is the best and most efficient organisational structure known in nature. Each element – each neuron – has the same constituency, but its level of influence varies dynamically according to the function of a specific movement. Every neuron is equally important in the fulfilment of their common mission of governing our lives.

Now, if science is so often inspired by nature in its applications, why not look at the complexity of the brain as our source of inspiration for a more balanced, efficient and sustainable organisational model? A useful tool would be to instil more discussion about the non-hierarchical models available, like peer-to-peer or wiki tools.

Therefore, in this "neural" structure, power is no longer organised in a structure where different categories are represented as being "above" or "below" or "at the same level". Rather, it is organised at a level where each category depends on each other and cannot function independently, thus abandoning the traditional pyramid format and turning into a network of multiple links and different levels of influence.

This new structure brings the need to implement our first suggested replacement of values: a movement towards Trust. This trust becomes crucial for Cooperation to be effective, so that the whole team/community can cooperate among them to achieve a common goal. Without trust, it is highly unlikely that individuals will cooperate willingly.

According to Kenneth Meyer[174], the neural structure of the mind and the body as a whole is a structure created by the pull of the DNA from birth and continues to operate under the "pull" of nature via electro-magnetic forces. Besides our own bodies, there is evidence of this throughout nature and the universe, like gravity and the pull of the sun as experienced by all the planets." Why not structure an organisation in a "pull structure" that is pulled by service purposes throughout the organisation?" he says. "This would be the ultimate sustainable organisation structure. The typical command and control structure with hierarchy is what he calls a push structure and it is why it is not very sustainable. Kenneth says that, by thinking in terms of "pull" and by measuring "pull", we can create "pull structures" for any organisation. This is why following a disaster, people "We all pulled together". When people work together, they "pull" together. That is also, why you do not hear the phrase "We all pushed together".

THE TRUST HORMONE

Recent behavioural evidence shows that the neuropeptide oxytocin increases trust among humans, offering a unique chance of gaining a deeper understanding of the neural mechanisms underlying trust and the adaptation to breach of trust[175]. A study by neuroscientist Thomas Baumgartner and colleagues at the University of Zurich in Switzerland, combines different disciplines and methodologies to investigate how the brain adapts to breaches of trust under the hypothesis that oxytocin plays an important role in the formation of trust. For example, the application of the hormone to investors in experimental games increased their tendency to engage in social risks and trust someone else with their money. The study highlights the neural mechanisms through which oxytocin acts to facilitate trust behaviour by investigating what happens in the brain when trust breaks down.

Moreover, the study demonstrates how oxytocin can facilitate social interactions after the violation of trust, by potentially lowering defence mechanisms associated with social risks and by overcoming negative feedback that is important for adapting behaviour in the future. It concludes that lower levels of oxytocin in some situations may certainly be adaptive, as a person will become more wary of possible harm, while higher levels of oxytocin may also be necessary at times to allow an individual to "forgive and forget," an imperative step in maintaining long-term relationships and mental well-being.

COLLECTIVISM AND HOLOGRAPHY

This new structure is also inspired in the concept of Collectivism and Holography, where a sense of community is used to reach an objective, without the use of rankings. Although this is illustrated in several organisations, it seems that the structure can only be maintained before the firms grow into large-scale ventures and when motivation is still driven by objectives and not financial results.

This holographic image works in a similar way to a kaleidoscope – one single object that contains many unique and collective individual shapes, which in the end come together to form a pattern. In essence, the concept of Holography – a form of Collectivism – uses the analogy of a hologram as the part that contains the whole, to suggest that organisations can become more "holographic". This happens if they abolish centralisation and foster a sense of the whole organisation among staff members, whereby employees actively takes part in the framing of the company's policy and vision, driving the organisational governance bottom-up.

As shown by Diniz and Handy on *Holographic Structures Creating Dynamic Governance for NGOs*[176], this structure tends to change as the organisations grow, gaining a more bureaucratic structure. Still, the authors believe that collectivist structures give employees and the community a chance to actively participate in core governance functions, creating "a tremendous flexibility" for the organisation, which can ultimately lead to long-lasting and long-term positive results. "The entire system is one of constant collaborations between staff, constituents, the executive and trustees" the paper reads. "The ideal situation within any governance process would be a balance of power dynamics so that no one stakeholder dominates the governance process", it adds.

"It always seems impossible until it's done". – Nelson Mandela

The Rio de Janeiro Carnaval in Brazil is a good example of the implementation of this holographic structure. The five-day event attracts over three million observers from all over the world, with over 500 teams of dancers and musicians in an event that requires a year's worth of work and mobilises over 500 thousand workers, involving an enormous supply chain.

Ultimately, Carnaval in Rio is considered as a democratic celebration where people from all social classes, races and genders get together to celebrate their culture with a common goal. As it happens with most organisations, the event grew into a well-organised parade, and now holds the statute of national institution, drawing hundreds of millions of dollars into the Brazilian economy every year. Carnaval groups born out of slum communities now find themselves signing corporate sponsorship deals worth millions of dollars, with some of Brazil's biggest brands clamouring to sponsor the event. If being a carnival queen or a dancer in a samba school was then a matter of community loyalty, now, some people receive money for their positions and some dancers even move around samba schools like professional footballers, Andre Skowronski, director of special projects for the União da Ilha Samba School, told Marketwatch[177]. "A top artistic director can demand up to 14,500 dollars per month", he explained.

Notwithstanding this, in its origin, Carnaval was a great example of a collective effort without a structured stratification. People gathered in their neighbourhoods to practice *samba* and created stands and costumes all year long, while musicians practiced their songs. All of this took place with no financial compensation involved, other than the satisfaction for creating such a big event and the consequent feeling of fulfilment that comes from taking part, as well as the possibility of winning the prize for the best performance[178,179].

The example of the organisation of the Rio de Janeiro Carnaval is the perfect illustration of another one of the key values we think must definitely integrate an organisational move towards cooperation: Passion & Optimism. Without passion, nobody can truly commit to anything and without optimism, positive outcomes become scarce.

THE RISK OF SCALING UP

Looking at this example, we conclude that organisations typically move towards a more bureaucratic – and hierarchical – model as they grow in scale, and this eventually leads to a substantial loss of community spirit and motivation, the values that were initially responsible for uniting the members of the community. Motivation then becomes driven by financial compensation, rather than by a sense of integration and achievement of a common goal.

CAN WE RELY ON OUR CAPABILITIES AND INFLUENCE INSTEAD OF RANKINGS AND TITLES?

As argued by Anderson and Brown in *The Functions and Dysfunctions of Hierarchy*[180], steeper hierarchies help groups succeed only when they are working on routine and simple tasks that do not require the opinions of a broad range of group members. Furthermore, they harm groups working on tasks that are more ambiguous and complex and that benefit from a wider range of group member judgements". Similarly, the authors propose that, "steeper hierarchies are more likely to lead to group failure when group leaders are corrupted by their power". Thus the maintenance of a community structure described as "neural", similar to the holographic structures proposed by Morgan in 1986[181], will effectively maintain the same purpose for all members of the community – working towards a common goal without focusing on competition, but rather on cooperation. As the organisation grows, it tends to gain a vertical structure, moving away from cooperation towards power and ranking, and changing the focus to that of a financial reward.

CAN PEOPLE PERFORM WITHOUT PRESSURE?

Abolishing hierarchies thus means that people would not have set roles or tasks, but rather that these are in line with their skills and the necessary performance at a given time. This brings the need for the third value: Versatility & Flexibility. Here, everyone can adopt a different role according to what is needed, integrated in flexible structures that adapt to the circumstances, in line with the description of the "neural" structure, where brain cells, originally with the same composition, relate to adapt to circumstances accordingly.

Additionally, the adoption of a collective approach towards the management of an organisation necessarily brings us to the "Multi-Peer Cooperation" (MPC) structure and the concept of peer-to-peer, whereby all peers dynamically increase or decrease their level of contribution and influence to the whole, and each peer connects with any other peer. The leader has the responsibility to align, empower, coordinate the whole network and extract the best of each member, understanding the members' capabilities and potential to empower and guide them into achieving the common goal.

COORDINATION PALADINS

Several organisations have adopted innovative structures through innovative CEOs. The early adopters of a different structure include Zappos, the online shoe and clothes shop run by CEO Tony Hsieh. The company took over headlines across the world when it went for a "no managers" approach, claiming it was going "holacratic". At the time, Hsieh described this new structure as a radical self-governing system where there are no job titles and no managers, a sort of "flatter" hierarchy where the company is composed of different circles, with "radical transparency" being the ultimate goal.

Darwin stated that, "it's not the fastest or strongest that survive. It's the ones most adaptive to change". In fact, Hsieh was already well-known for his take on human capital and motivation. "Your personal core values define who you are, and a company's core values ultimately define the company's character and brand. For individuals, character is destiny. For organisations, culture is destiny", he said.

Hsieh's approach strongly shows the importance of the fourth driver we suggest in the move towards cooperation: Empowerment & Mentoring. Through empowerment and mentoring, employees receive the necessary skills and follow-up to optimise their progress and are capable of adapting to new situations and adopting new roles.

The US-based Treehouse, a company claiming to have revolutionised "how people learn web design, web development and iOS development", is also an example of the followers of Zappos' approach, with the successful adoption of a new structure[182]. The company is largely remote and offers employees four-day workweeks, among other benefits. However, what makes it stand out is the fact that it has recently opted for a completely flat organisational chart, with all middle management removed. "No one reports to anyone", co-founders Alan Johnson and Ryan Carson, say. The way the company works is, it organises around projects proposed by employees, using collaboration software. The employees propose the projects they want to see completed and, if enough co-workers join in, they can get started.

Since switching to the no-manager structure, Carson says he gets less than twenty emails a day and believes worker morale has skyrocketed. According to Carson, the main tenet is to treat people, as he wants to be treated. "We all should be able to make adult decisions and take care of ourselves. Everything comes from there pretty easily", he says. He goes on to say that, he sees the "no-manager company" as an ant colony. "It looks really chaotic and it is sometimes hard to understand what is happening, but then a crazy structure gets built. Often, even as the CEO, I do not understand exactly what is happening on any one day. (...) It is not really in the best interest of Treehouse or any company for the CEOs to truly control its direction, because he is just one guy or girl". He summarises the outcome of this organisational change with the sentence: "It's up to everyone to make themselves happy and make sure that they are enjoying their job. And if they don't, then they can leave". This method tends to produce positive outcomes, as the responsibility of each member of the team is to achieve his/her own happiness. Naturally, when we are happy, we will also want to make people around us happy!

Furthermore, Treehouse is going further afield in other sectors, namely transparency. "We're thinking about exposing everyone's salary, but that's only because it will help everybody make a decision. For instance, if you want to set up a project and you add a bunch of people to it, you should have some sort of idea as to the cost of that".

A similar approach is that of high-performance teams (HPTs), a concept within organisation development referring to teams, organisations or virtual groups that are highly focused on their goals and that achieve superior business results. High-performance teams outperform all other similar teams and they outperform expectations given their composition. HPTs can be defined as groups of people with specific roles and complementary talents and skills, aligned with and committed to a common purpose. They consistently show high levels of collaboration and innovation that produce superior results. Within the HPT, people are highly skilled and are able to interchange their roles.

Furthermore, leadership within the team is not vested in a single individual. Instead, various team members take on the leadership role, according to the need at that moment in time. HPTs have robust methods of resolving conflict efficiently, so that conflict does not become a roadblock to achieving the team's goals. There is a sense of clear focus and intense energy within a high-performance team.

"He who loses his individuality loses all". – Mahatma Gandhi

A CHANGE OF VALUES

The adoption of this different and innovative "neural" structure necessarily entails a move from the traditional competition-based structure towards a structure based on cooperation – the very aspect that defines the "neural" functioning. That is why we propose the driving forces of change & trust, versatility &

flexibility, passion & optimism and empowerment & mentoring to become the core values of any organisation.

Albeit essential, these values do not appear on their own. Rather, they are a result of all the values mentioned above: an employee that is given the trust to act according to each situation, take on responsibilities, given feedback and mentoring, is more likely to be passionate about his/her job. Therefore, the proposal is that companies move from a spirit of competition to a dynamic in cooperation, through the adoption and focus on four core values: trust, versatility and flexibility, empowerment and mentoring, passion and optimism. All of these values are intertwined and interdependent and thus each of them is essential for the other to succeed.

REINFORCING COOPERATION

To illustrate the application of this shift towards Cooperation, we have chosen to use the analogy of an orchestra to represent the perfect cooperative organisation. In an orchestra, this cooperation needs to be present at all times, and the figure of the maestro does not represent a boss, but rather a coordinator, who is capable of empowering the most of each musician – through Empowerment and Mentoring, and who is inspiring rather than imposing. The members of the orchestra are led by their Passion for what they do and foster a feeling of mutual Trust that enables them to coordinate with each other, using Versatility and Flexibility to adapt to each different piece they play or the people who will integrate the orchestra on a given occasion.

DO WE REALLY NEED COMPETITION?

In the words of conductor Benjamin Zander on *The Art of Possibility*[183], "if we describe revenge, pride, fear and self-righteousness as the villains – and people as the hope – we will come together to create possibility". That is to say, only cooperation can truly enable the attainment of an objective.

Therefore, replacing Competitiveness with Cooperation, both at an internal and external level, will enable organisations to move towards an economy-oriented model. Here, organisations are evaluated by their full economic value – their impact on the market and the communities, through the value of their actions, products and services, as well as the economic value of the internal community; in other words, the wellbeing of the members of the organisation.

Thus, in the same way that a maestro gains recognition by his/her work resulting reputation and bearing in mind that this performance is based on the maestro's work in close coordination with the orchestra or the team, the sustainable organisation follows a model based on full aggregated economic value rather than competitiveness between organisations in the same market. Therefore, the company has an impact in the market and the communities through the value of its products and services, as well as the economic value of its internal community – providing happiness and fulfilment to all its members.

"What you can do, we cannot do, and what we can do, you cannot do, but together we can do something beautiful". – Mother Teresa

To illustrate the set of changes we propose, we have chosen a set of characteristics throughout the four main points that make up the proposal for an organisation to become and remain truly sustainable. In this chapter, we propose a shift from Competitiveness to Cooperation. Thus, the aim is to implement the shift of the following characteristics on the left (related to the Old Economy) towards the characteristics on the right (related to the New Economy, and the Sustainable Organisations):

OLD ECONOMY		SUSTAINABLE ORGANISATION	
Victory	The leader aims to succeed and become victorious.	Fulfilment	The leader aims to attain an objective for the good of his company and society as a whole.
Power	The leader represents an image of power and control; money is criterion to demonstrate and influence power.	Recognition	The leader gains a natural recognition, respect and admiration by his/her capability, knowledge, influence and performance.
Ranking	The organisation is highly stratified in structures of power, where some are "above" and others "below"; an artificial system to impose respect, filter the flow of knowledge and submission.	Inter-dependence	The organisation is organised with interdependent categories, dynamic levels of influence, equally necessary to reach the proposed objectives.
Loss	The goal of succeeding is opposed to the fear of losing. The situation is win versus lose.	Motivation	The aim is a win-win situation, ruled by a motivation to improve the society as a whole.

OLD ECONOMY		SUSTAINABLE ORGANISATION	
Envy	The structures of power implement a sense of envy, a destructive feeling permanently nurtured among members, caused by the desire to get more power.	Admiration	A community works together as a team to reach the proposed objectives and receive common recognition.
Work	Obligation, detachment, schedule, formality, functionality and wage.	Take part and play	Involvement, being part of something, contribution, flexibility, versatility, recognition and reward.
Struggle	Lack of motivation; lack of recognition; no sense of fulfilment.	Enjoyment	Motivation to work and to be part of the project; happiness with the results and performance by the team.

The set of words on the left emphasises the internal climate within most organisations, which leads people to see work as a sacrifice rather than an enjoyable and stimulating activity. The set of words on the right represents a performance undertaken to achieve a common goal and coordination within the community that provides motivation and a sense of achievement through recognition and fulfilment.

While for some, this can seem merely utopic, we truly believe that, in organisations formed by intelligent and fair people, this evolution from competitiveness to cooperation can be fulfilling and healthy. It has been proven that happy people tend to live longer and healthier lives and it has been demonstrated that most satisfying emotions are free, and thus impossible to buy, be it with money or power. Happiness can be contagious!

Now, the challenge is to measure each of these characteristics…

2 – FROM AUTHORITY TO RECOGNITION

"Mediocrity knows nothing higher than itself; but talent instantly recognises genius." – Arthur Conan Doyle in The Valley of Fear

"Don't worry when you are not recognised, but strive to be worthy of recognition." – Abraham Lincoln

"I do not believe in immortality of the individual, and I consider ethics to be an exclusively human concern with no superhuman authority behind it." – Albert Einstein

"He who establishes his argument by noise and command shows that his reason is weak." – Michel de Montaigne

"The ultimate authority must always rest with the individual's own reason and critical analysis." – Dalai Lama

"Anyone who conducts an argument by appealing to authority is not using his intelligence, he is just using his memory." – Leonardo Da Vinci

"No man has any natural authority over his fellow men." – Jean-Jacques Rousseau

"Once in society, the desire for approbation – or, henceforth, the desire for recognition – comes to regulate all human conduct." – Adam Smith, Scottish philosopher

"Never let anyone come to you without coming away better and happier." – Mother Teresa

MERCENARIES AND MISSIONARIES

Carthage fought hard for 23 years against Rome and finally sued for peace in 241 BC. Sicily rendered to the Romans and the Punic troops stationed there. Meanwhile, the renowned general Hamilcar Barca was removed from this post and was replaced by the Carthaginian Gisco, who was to organise the evacuation and pay of the mercenaries. So, the mercenaries slowly began arriving by ship, expecting to receive their rewards for their years of service, among them the Libyan infantry, Numidian and Mauretanian light cavalry, Celts, light-armed Iberians, armoured Greeks and Campanians, Ligurians and Balearic slingers, as well as Roman deserts and many others.

The list was endless, but these mercenaries did not make up a coherent army, but rather a group of nomads on the move who could hardly communicate between them due to their different origins. The only thing they shared was the desire to obtain a payment when they fulfilled their tasks. Still, this could be considered as one of the first professional armies in the world and like any army, there were deeply-rooted hierarchies, which were also strongly characterised by the importance and use of authority, relations of power that rule the way each tier of the organisation works and behaves.

The Romans were also famous for making use of mercenaries wherever possible and Genghis Khan, also resorted to the use of mercenaries in the 12th century in his planned expansion across the world. Centuries later, mercenaries were still being used, namely in France, Spain, Portugal, Germany and the UK and today, the private military company (PMC) is recognised as a contemporary strand of the mercenary trade, showing the activity is still present at a global level.

In fact, mercenaries are one of the oldest operating professions in the world, so it is no wonder that they are enrooted in management so deeply. In this part, we will use the analogy of Mercenaries to represent the traditional image of top management in traditional organisations, the exact opposite to the image of the ideal leader in the New Economy's organisations. We will compare them to the concept of

Missionaries – the exact opposite of Mercenaries – considering their motivation and reward.

Looking at the definition of the very word "mercenary", it is also easy to note how it can be applied to a wide range of activities. A mercenary is not simply "a professional soldier hired to serve in a foreign army", as quoted by Oxford Dictionaries. It has come to mean "someone primarily motivated by personal gain" and "making money at the expense of ethics". Taking the latter definitions into account, we believe the "mercenary" would be the perfect analogy – or even the definition – of the executives of the Old Economy.

Missionaries, on the other hand, are people sent out on a religious mission with the sole purpose of spreading knowledge about their religion and without any financial interest whatsoever. Missionaries tend to be less famous than mercenaries, probably due to the essence of their goal. The word has come to acquire a wider meaning and now regards anyone that is strongly in favour of a project, a set of principles and values, and who tries to persuade others.

A good example would be David Livingstone, best known for his accomplishments as an explorer. He was the first man to map Africa and the first European to discover many areas of Africa, but what is less known is that Livingstone was also a missionary in Africa, where he lived for 30 years. He travelled over 29,000 miles preaching the gospel, providing medical services (due to his training as a doctor), building churches, and mapping the vast African continent. In his journal[184], written late in life, he wrote about his work as a missionary: "People talk of the sacrifice I have made in spending so much time in Africa. (…) It is emphatically no sacrifice. Say rather it is a privilege".

This comparison between mercenaries and missionaries is nothing new. Venture capitalist John Doerr[185] had already described the leaders of the Old Economy as mercenaries, contrasting them with the leaders of the New Economy – driven by new values and goals – which he argues need to become missionaries rather than mercenaries[186]. John Doerr explains: "Mercenaries think opportunistically; missionaries think strategically. Mercenaries go for the sprint; missionaries go for the marathon. Mercenaries focus on their competitors and financial statements; missionaries focus on their customers and value statements. Mercenaries are bosses of wolf packs; missionaries are mentors or coaches of teams. Mercenaries worry about entitlements; missionaries are obsessed with making a contribution. Mercenaries are motivated by the lust for making money; missionaries, while recognising the importance of money, are fundamentally driven by the desire to make meaning".

THE ROLE OF TRANSPARENCY

Successful management entails making difficult decisions that involve sacrifices, but as explained in the previous chapter, the success of these decisions often depends on a strongly collaborative process characterised by a high degree of transparency. In the case of mercenaries, this transparency is not a key element. As mentioned above, the "members" are not familiar with each other and are united by a common goal, although the achievement of this goal does not necessarily go through a collaborative effort.

However, the case of missionaries is entirely different: they fight for a cause that is disclosed in a transparent manner from the very beginning and taken through a process of collaborating with a team, which is driven by the same desire to achieve the stated objective. In *The Collaboration Imperative*[187], which examines how managers can better unlock the best of their organisations, Cisco executives Ron Ricci and Carl Wiese, wrote that, "When you are open and transparent about the answers to three questions – who made the decision, who is accountable for the outcomes of the decision and is that accountability real – people in organisations spend far less time questioning how or why a decision was made. Think of how much time is wasted ferreting out details when a decision is made and communicated because the people who are affected don't know who made the decision or who is accountable for its consequences".

"Truth nourishes the soul. Untruth corrodes it." – Mahatma Gandhi

This transparency has thus become essential in making sure that the "team" follows the spirit and the letter of a certain decision. In big organisations of the New Economy, it is now a crucial motivational tool. It is thus important that everyone understands why something is being done and the value of doing that thing, so that the team becomes the advocate of the objective, rather than the elements that help achieve it. This can be done through the key principle explained in the previous chapter – cooperation.

In *The Truth About Transparency*[188] by Paul D. Meyer, organisational transparency is a key element to create trust among stakeholders, as it encourages more informed decision making and supports greater participation. He sees the need for transparency as consequence of the digital age – which strongly instilled the New Economy – and the subsequent "digital generations" who no longer tolerate not being able to access any kind of information. Thus, this transparency is being hailed as the new competitive advantage, Meyer states, "the new mantra for leadership", citing Eric Ooi Lip Aun, executive director of the consulting firm PWC Malaysia, who said that improved financial transparency within publicly held organisations could increase stock price by as much as 25%. According to Meyer, if we consider this, then we need to consider that this transparency could also bring similar results in terms of recruitment and involvement.

Furthermore, Meyer recognises that transparency and trust are inextricably connected – transparency is a means to a trusting environment and increased transparency helps develop a culture characterised by trust, a culture that is satisfying and enjoyable to join and participate in. However, just as this transparency brings positive opportunities, it also presents several challenges, Meyer points out, as it creates organisational vulnerabilities. Still, as reputation is often an organisation's most valuable asset, commitment to transparency defines the reputation of an organisation.

KNOWLEDGE & INFLUENCE

"If I had asked people what they wanted, they would have said faster, horses". – Henry Ford

The concept of authority has also been criticised as being used to hide a lack of knowledge and a lack of capacity to influence people. When a leader is able to demonstrate a deep knowledge of the business and the organisation, it becomes more likely that he/she will also be able to effectively influence and inspire the team. To this effect, great leaders have to understand their business, as well as the people that are part of their project—their moods, their needs, their expectations. This is bound to make them feel connected with the leader.

Hence, because the leader is the primary element when it comes to leadership and management in any organisation, it is paramount that he/she has a strong knowledge and established skills in a wide range of areas. This can provide a foundation from which this leader can contribute with these skills, adapted to the nature, industry and environment of the said organisation.

> CAN'T WE JUST TRUST AND BE EVENTUALLY DISAPPOINTED INSTEAD OF NEVER BE DISAPPOINTED AND NEVER SENSE TRUST?

However, the New Economy has more often been associated with a lack of transparency, also often associated with positions of authority, lack of trust and strong competitiveness. Thus, when moving away from the authority of the mercenaries to the recognition of the missionaries, this transparency becomes a key element to establish a position of trust, an essential element in the list of values that need to be present for a successful shift towards sustainability. Without full transparency, this cannot be achieved. Transparency and the consequential accountability necessarily bring a positive outlook on the firm.

RESPECT & RECOGNITION

When allying this knowledge to the aforementioned transparency, the result is necessarily a sense of respect, which positively contributes towards the general reputation of the organisation and the reputation of the leader. A leader can only gain respect from his/her employees if he/she is able to prove that, the organisation is transparent and that he/she has the necessary knowledge to be competent enough to take on that role. Similarly, only when a leader is respected by the team, can the leader truly influence the team and gain resulting recognition.

As the saying goes, "respect is earned, fear is imposed". It is the job of the leader to work towards attaining this respect and thus retain the motivation of his/her team, rather than have them work for the fear of losing their job. Furthermore, this sense of respect entails a wider sphere, outside the company itself. In the words of the philosopher Hobbes, "… the value or worth of a man is, as of all other things, his price – that is to say, so much as would be given for the use of his power – and therefore is not absolute but a thing dependent on the need and judgement of another". That is to say, gaining respect does not come automatically and it is something that needs to be maintained through the leader's efforts of motivating his team and keeping them involved.

"Power based on love is a thousand times more effective and permanent than one derived from fear and punishment" – *Mahatma Gandhi*

Mike Myatt, leadership advisor to Fortune 500 CEOs and their Boards of Directors, has been widely regarded as America's Top CEO Coach. In this regard, he notes that respect is paramount for leaders as they instil loyalty in their "team" as both these elements go hand-in-hand. In fact, he believes that the lack of loyalty undermines the sustainability of the position of a leader, as it makes it short-lived. He said that, "while successful leaders share many common traits, all great leaders have one thing in common – they are not only not adept at earning the loyalty of those they lead, but they also recognise that loyalty is a two-way street. When it comes to loyalty, the simple rule is that you will not receive what you will not give".

Therefore, leaders who create a fear-based culture will have employees who don't give them their best and who run away when things turn out bad. In contrary, CEOs who try to act as "inspirational servants, catalysts, teachers and team builders" will follow the following principles based on valuing the opinions of their team and encouraging scrutiny, encouraging interaction between the team members and with their superiors through measures like the 360 review process. He concludes: "What is rightfully earned and freely given (loyalty, trust and respect) will always outlast what is imprudently acquired for the wrong reasons (the bully tactics of fear-based control)".

William George is a professor of management practice at Harvard Business School, where he teaches leadership development and ethics. He is also the former Chairman and CEO of Medtronic. In an article published by Fast Company[189], he says that the key to create altruistic organisations that can transform society and the economy is a compassionate and authentic leadership. "We need a new generation of leaders to step forward and provide this new kind of leadership", he says.

George's reasoning is that not only this compassionate and authentic leadership is a good thing to have, but it is also necessary for a healthy society. "I believe that they [his generation of leaders] have failed in their responsibility. As a result of the failures of leadership in the last decade, there has been a loss of confidence in our leaders, and a loss of trust. Each of us who takes a leadership role has a responsibility to the people we serve", he says.

He goes on to provide the example of Medtronic, which was measured not by earnings per share, but by how many people it helped. "My greatest source of pride is that in the time I was there, we went from 300,000 people per year to 10 million people per year who were being restored to fuller, more active lives", he explains. "We always tried to convey this meaning to the people in the company, because that's what inspired them, not the stock price, not the earnings".

George believes that the role of the leader is definitely not to exert power, as it suggests a situation where those who give power, have less. Rather, he believes that leadership is about empowering people to lead, which can result in stronger organisations.

"Arrogance really comes from insecurity, and in the end our feeling that we are bigger than others is really the flip side of our feeling that we are smaller than others" – Desmond Tutu

COMMITMENT

In a sustainable organisation where the leader commits to the organisation's objective through transparently disclosing that objective and encouraging cooperation and action by the team, this commitment also becomes a key element. After all, if there is transparency, then everyone contributes, understands and naturally commits to the objectives and goals.

This commitment equals a dedication to an organisation, cause or belief and a willingness to get involved: people who are truly committed to an organisation believe this organisation is important and they follow through the mission of the said organisation, sticking with it. The more people can be encouraged by this commitment, the better the performance will be.

In addition, this commitment is important for several reasons. First, the more committed people are, the better they can influence others to take on this commitment. In the end, this commitment takes cooperation to a higher level, as it fosters involvement, cooperation and trust – all of these key elements for the sustainability of any organisation. Furthermore, commitment follows the successful implementation of the principles explained above, as they are all interlinked. So, people will only feel committed when they work together, when they are clear about what they are working for and when they respect the cause – and the leader.

If someone is not fully committed to a job, it is very unlikely that this person will achieve his/her best result. Similarly, when showing the utmost commitment, the CEO is able to use knowledge to influence the team, the transparency to foster respect, and this is bound to turn the CEO into an inspirational figure for the whole team – the much sought-after recognition.

SUSTAINABILITY PALADINS

There have been several examples of "missionary" CEOs who have tried to become agents of change in malfunctioning companies. One example is Michael Woodford, praised for his courage and perseverance when he became the CEO of Japanese Camera manufacturer, Olympus. Already, it was uncommon to have a British person lead a Japanese conglomerate, but what he did when he stepped in was even more unheard of. Woodford described Olympus' corporate culture as an "emperor system" and a "regime" and he got a lot of attention when he was fired in early 2011 for exposing US$1.7 billion in accounting irregularities. His investigation into the accounting debacle led to the firing of the Chairman of the board (the very one who had hired him), along with two senior executives. Although the outcome was unfortunate for Woodford, he showed his missionary spirit when he decided to reveal a situation he knew would not be well accepted within the board, but that was seen as necessary through his own principles. Woodford is the perfect example of the adoption of the key value of Transparency.

"A good leader can engage in a debate frankly and thoroughly, knowing that at the end he and the other side must be closer, and thus emerge stronger. You don't have that idea when you are arrogant, superficial, and uninformed." – Nelson Mandela

Another example of a tenacious CEO is Chrysler's Sergio Marchionne. When the Italian-Canadian stepped in, Chrysler was in bad shape. Marchionne took on the role of a true leader when he devoted himself to the cause of saving Chrysler. His focused leadership led to a 23% increase in Chrysler, Dodge, Ram and Jeep sales and total sales hit the roof, compared to 2009, when the company had billions in debt. Here, Marchionne was capable of exerting another of the driving forces we believe are crucial to attain sustainability: Knowledge & Influence.

SHOULD KNOWLEDGE BE FREE AND ACCESSIBLE?

McKinsey's & Company's published report on the role of the CEO[190] gives the example of Gandhi's famous edict: "For things to change, first I must change". That is to say, it is up to the CEO to dictate and show the change he/she wants to see in the company and its members. It gives the example of N. R. Narayana Murthy, the Chairman of the board and former CEO of India's Infosys, who believes the responsibility of the leader, is to "create mental energy among people so that they enthusiastically embrace the transformation". His decision in 2002 to take on the job title of chief mentor at Infosys meant that he had to reinvent himself. He explained, at the time: "You have to sacrifice yourself for a big cause before you can ask others to do the same", much in the same way as missionaries sacrifice themselves towards their goals. Here, the CEO was able to gain **Respect** from his **Commitment** to create a more satisfying environment to employees, which gave him the resulting **Recognition**.

In *How the Best Leaders Build Trust*[191], Stephen M. R. Covey gives the example of Warren Buffet, the CEO of Berkshire Hathaway who completed a major acquisition of McLane Distribution (a US$23 billion company) from Wal-Mart. As public companies, both Berkshire Hathaway and Wal-Mart are subject to all kinds of scrutiny. Therefore, a merger of this size would typically take a long time to complete and cost several millions of dollars, but in this instance, because both parties operated with high trust, the deal was made with one two-hour meeting and a handshake and was completed in less than a month.

Many other leaders have discussed the importance of trust, mostly recognising that it is a key element in management. In *Trust: The Best Way to Manage*[192], Reinhard K. Sprenger cites the example of former PepsiCo CEO Craig Weatherup. "People will tolerate honest mistakes, but if you violate their trust you will find it very difficult to regain their confidence. That is one reason that you need to treat trust as your most precious asset", he said.

THE "NEW ECONOMY" LEADER

We believe that, to take the mercenaries out of managers and turn them into missionaries, there is again the need for a shift in values, from this ruling of power relations to relationships characterised by recognition and inspiration. This entails a shift based on four elements that relate to the relationships present within the company – transparency, knowledge & influence, respect and commitment.

IS ANYONE BORN WITH A TITLE?

Furthermore, we believe that what we call the New Economy leader – one that fully complies with the needs of a new economy – will necessarily embody all the aforementioned values. Acknowledging that there is a dire need to move to a new style of management, a result of a changing economy, we recognise the need for a top-down change, where transparency helps and forces CEOs to give the example to the rest of the community, creating this sense of respect and recognition.

This change could also result in the empowerment of meritocracy, where power is invested in individuals almost exclusively according to merit, based on intellectual talent and demonstrated achievements. In fact, the meritocratic governance model[193], a commonly found model in which participants gain influence over a project through the recognition of their contributions, could be applied here. A famous example of this is the Apache Software Foundation (ASF) which operates with an almost completely "flat" structure, which means that anyone willing to contribute can engage with their projects at any level.

The flatness of a meritocratic project's structure comes from the fact that once someone has decision-making authority, they have exactly the same authority as everyone else. Another aspect of this flatness is that decision making responsibilities are usually reserved for those willing and able to understand, and appropriately represent the views of the wider community. So, when an important decision is made, those with a vote are expected to represent the views of those who have yet to earn a vote.

"It is better to lead from behind and to put others in front, especially when you celebrate victory when nice things occur. You take the front line when there is danger. Then people will appreciate your leadership." – Nelson Mandela

In *The Meritocracy Myth*[194], Stephen J. McNamee and Robert K. Miller, Jr. argue that there is a gap between how people think the system works and how the system actually does work, to which they refer as "the meritocracy myth" or the myth that the system distributes resources according to the merit of individuals. The authors challenge this assertion by suggesting that, while merit does affect who ends up with what, its impact is vastly overestimated. Moreover, they identify a series of non-merit factors that suppress, neutralise or even negate the effects of merit and create barriers to individual mobility.

Furthermore, they argue that societal resources are not distributed on the basis of individual merit, due to the combined effects of non-merit factors such as inheritance, social and cultural advantages, unequal education opportunities, luck and the changing structure of job opportunities. Hence, they do believe the system can operate more closely according to meritocratic principles and suggest this can be done in four ways. First, they suggest that current forms of discrimination can decrease or disappear entirely. Secondly, they suggest that the wealthy could be encouraged to redistribute greater amounts of their accumulated wealth through philanthropy and thirdly, they suggest the tax system should be redesigned to become genuinely progressive in ways that would close the distance between those at the top and the bottom of the system. Finally, they suggest that more government resources are allocated to provide more equal access to critical services such as education and healthcare.

While we believe these external factors are crucial in the empowerment of meritocracy in this New Economy, they are external and thus, they cannot be controlled within the organisation, with the exception of the second suggestion, which goes hand-in-hand with our "Marginal Million Theory". What we are proposing is an organisational change that can then be transposed to the external economic context, affecting the population as a whole.

Here, it is also important to mention the principle of corporate governance, the system by which corporations are directed and controlled. The governance structure specifies the distribution of rights and responsibilities among different participants in the corporation and specifies the rules and procedures for making decisions in corporate affairs. Governance provides the structure through which corporations set and pursue their objectives, whilst reflecting the context of the social, regulatory and market environment, monitoring actions, policies and decisions of these corporations. Across Continental Europe and Japan, a similar model is used – called coordinated or multi-tasker – which recognises the interests of workers, managers, suppliers, customers and the community.

Thus, moving from authority to recognition necessarily implies a set of changes. By allying this sense of community and cooperation to rewards in compliance with a median, the longevity of the company, community size and innovation whilst avoiding and penalising speculation (as mentioned in the previous chapter), the company can truly create something useful to benefit its customers. In turn, this will create a cooperative effort to stay at the top, followed by the resulting recognition. It will also replace the concept of "wage" by that of "reward" ('wage' as the contractual salary for a given position, and 'reward' as an incentive based on performance), balancing it in a way that ends the current reality: the top is getting wealthier at the expense of all the rest. Finally, the "win versus loose" perspective is also replaced by a "win-win" corporate focus – what we call "courting to win". As a result, the leader gains the status of an agent of change.

Again, taking the example of an orchestra and considering that, in a sustainable organisation, the conductor gains a reputation due to his coordination with the members of the orchestra, his/her image is not based on the orchestra's compensation and profits, but rather on the recognition, motivation and respect gained from the performance of the maestro.

Thinking about leadership, the same principle applies. Recognition, motivation and respect are the true originators of security, opportunity and harmony, and all these values come as crucial for the wellbeing of the company and its employees. Thus, a leader that is recognised and respected will necessarily have more value than a leader who earns a valuable sum. In the same way, without showing transparency, the leader will not be respected, there will be no trust, and the CEO will not succeed in influencing the team/community.

What we are proposing is that organisations foster the presence of leaders who, much like Woodford and Marchionne, are motivated by a mission rather than by a compensation that does not look at the means to achieve an end. In other words, we are proposing leaders that act as conductors, that trust the team, that are able to delegate, teach and lead by example. A leader that fosters transparency, knowledge, influence and respect is necessarily motivated by values. In turn, these will be passed on to the team, the employees. Finally, working in an environment characterised by such principles necessarily leads the whole team to perform better, be more motivated and happier.

Similar to the previous chapter, we have chosen a set of keywords throughout this point to illustrate a sustainable organisation in the shift "From Authority to Recognition". Therefore, the aim is to implement the following shifts:

OLD ECONOMY		*SUSTAINABLE ORGANISATION*	
Delegate	The leader merely delegates tasks to employees to achieve his set goals.	Involve, mentor	The leader contributes to a community effort to achieve an objective.
Command	The leader assumes an authoritative position and coordinates the different ranked positions accordingly.	Mobilise, Inspire	The leader coordinates the efforts of his community in a dependable manner so that they all cooperate.

	OLD ECONOMY		**SUSTAINABLE ORGANISATION**	
Capture	The leader takes the recognition from the objectives attained by the whole company.	Empower	The leader shares the value created with his employees and gives them merit.
Power	The "mercenary" CEO is a leader and strives on power through the command of his employees.	Guiding, Team, "Band of brothers"...	The leader behaves as a member of a team, a coordinator, necessary only to the synchronisation of his team.
Obligation	The leader conveys a sense of obligation to the employees; they are merely doing the job they are paid for.	Happiness, commitment, complicity	The leader motivates and makes employees want to strive without any direction to do so; they want to be part of a project and want to do their best to go beyond the set goals.
Task	Every part of a job is a forceful step to keep the job.	Fulfilment, Involvement	The attainment of a goal is motivation and leads to a sense of fulfilment for having been part of success.
Individualism	The leader sees company performance because of his image and presence and ignores the merit of his team.	Empowerment, Purpose	The leader empowers the team to take on a stronger presence in the company's projects.

The set of words on the left describes the typical "mercenary" leadership that is still found in most organisations, encouraged by the principles of the Old Economy, which fostered an environment of power and forced leadership. The set of words on the right represents the leadership of the New Economy, which is led by a "mission" to improve the general performance of the organisation, while involving the team and sharing their success, leading to happier employees, in a more stable company.

3 – FROM UNFAIR WAGES TO FAIR REWARDING

"I feel fine with people making a lot of money for doing a great job. (...) If you flop, why in the world should you be making US$5 million a year, or US$3 million a year? Pay for performance is fine. Pay for showing up is not". – Warren Buffett

"Incentives should be large enough to provide an occasion for celebrating success but not so large as to distort behaviour. And incentives can include recognition and things other than money. Companies get themselves into trouble all the time by being too clever with their incentives". – Jeffrey Pfeffer, Professor of Organizational Behaviour at Stanton University

"Managers receiving hundreds of thousands a year — and setting their compensation for themselves – are not being paid wages, they are appropriating surplus value in the guise of wages". – Michael Harrington, writer political activist and theorist

"If one can get fired for poor performance, one must also be able to "get rich" for extraordinary performance". – Peter F. Drucker

"Few people- and probably no one outside the executive suite – sees much reason for these very large executive compensations. There is little correlation between them and company performance". – Peter F. Drucker, The Frontiers of Management (1986)

"This is America. We don't disparage wealth. We don't begrudge anybody for achieving success," Obama said. "But what gets people upset — and rightfully so — are executives being rewarded for failure. Especially when those rewards are subsidized by U.S. taxpayers". – Barack Obama

"We are taking the air out of golden parachutes". – Barack Obama

"Peace without justice is an impossibility". – Desmond Tutu

Executive and workers' compensation has always been a hot topic and this debate goes back to the early 1900s. In *Back to the Future: A Century of Compensation*[195], George T. Milkovich and Jennifer Stevens cited a 1939 report on US President Roosevelt's call for caps on executive salaries and public reporting of the compensation of the top people in public companies, proving that the scepticism over executive compensation is far from being a recent topic. Earlier, in the 1890s, Colonel Procter from Procter and Gamble announced his belief that profit sharing, pensions, a week's vacation with pay after two years of experience and employment security increased "efficiency and loyalty".

The authors conclude that although the management of compensation has gained more importance since the 1900s, it is still far from being sustainable. For the situation to improve, they suggest ending the search for a right strategy and ascertaining that compensation systems will continue to change and the best solution is to adjust by improving our understanding of the circumstances.

The current compensation practices could be broadly described using the analogy of a bus. The passengers of the bus are important, but they are passive, and the bus driver is the only active element and thus the one that should be compensated accordingly (even though this does not necessarily happen in real life). Although the passengers and the bus driver represent the "team" in the bus, there is no actual coordination to achieve an end, and the bus driver is the only element that needs to make an effort to reach an end – taking the passengers to the predefined destinations.

Similarly, most traditional corporate practices involve highly paid top managers with a "team" that tends to have a set of tasks they need to complete which are as crucial as the managers' tasks, although this "team" tends to be considered as passive in terms of their mobility, flexibility, recognition and compensation. This happens because they are not treated as key elements to achieve a goal and their compensation is not treated as a key part of their motivation to complete that achievement. In fact, this is considered as one of the most damaging facts to the sustainability of an organisation: the fact that executive compensation demonstrates a feeble relation with executive performance, which has been widely debated among executives, the media and academics alike.

When it comes to the average employee's compensation, this tends to be linked to the concept of "wage" rather than "reward". It is the most common type of earning and constitutes the core element in income for most active people.

PAY IS NOT LINKED TO PERFORMANCE

Bestselling author and journalist Malcolm Gladwell, who specialises in the unexpected implications of research in social sciences, has been one of the critics. In an article published in the New York Times[196], he stated that, "a few years ago, a group of economists looked at more than a hundred of Fortune 500 firms, trying to figure out what predicted how much money the CEO made. Compensation, it turned out, was only weakly related to the size and profitability of the company. What really mattered was how much money the members of the compensation committee of the board of directors made in their jobs".

The author concluded: "Pay is not determined vertically, in other words, according to the characteristics of the organisation an executive works for; it is determined horizontally, according to the characteristics of the executive's peers. They decide, among themselves, what the right amount is. This is not a market".

Here, Gladwell recognises that the determination of executive pay is not related to the performance of the executive or the performance of the company itself. This goes hand in hand with the realisation that many executives receive compensation packages that are considered as "outrageous" and "unjustifiable" in detriment to the "passengers of the bus".

An article posted on Knowledge@Wharton[197], a University of Pennsylvania blog, points out some examples of excessive executive compensation and lavish perks. The publication by the Wharton faculty defends that "executives cannot afford to remain tone-deaf about the appearance of large packages and perks at a time when taxpayers are being asked to finance banks and corporations while their own savings shrink and their jobs are at risk".

When it was disclosed that New York financial executives took in US$18.4 billion in bonuses while the banking system was receiving billions in a taxpayer-funded bailout, President Obama said: "It is shameful. [The people] who are asking for help [need] to show some restraint, discipline and... sense of responsibility", but executives did not seem to take any shame for it and nothing has changed since then. However, the president announced a set of executive compensation limits aimed at firms receiving federal aid under the Troubled Asset Relief Program (TARP), which place a US$500,000 cap on salaries.

There are abundant examples of CEOs who have received whopping compensations. In 2012, the CEO of Oracle, Lawrence J. Ellison, received US$96 million in compensation over the year, making him the highest-paid CEO over that year. Apple's Tim Cook led the list in 2011 with an annual compensation of US$378 million, justified by a stock package that vests over a decade. Meanwhile, at Wynn Resorts, CEO Steve Wynn enjoyed over a million dollars' worth of personal travel on his company's private jet. At Hertz, CEO Mark Frissora spent nearly half a million dollars also travelling on the corporate jet.

"Fair means can alone produce fair results". – Mahatma Gandhi

For the 100 highest-paid CEOs among American companies, with revenues of over US$5 billion, the typical 2012 perks package went up by 18.7% from 2011, according to an analysis by The Times, in line with the rise in overall cash compensation. "I think it is offensive", says Charles M. Elson, director of the John L. Weinberg Center for Corporate Governance at the University of Delaware. "The corporate aircraft is for a business purpose; it's a business tool. You don't take the company car to Disneyland with your kids, so why would you use a corporate jet for personal use?"

The expert adds we should not expect executives to give up their prized benefits anytime soon, even if shareholders can now publicly register their displeasure. "If I ask for it and you give it to me, then why not ask? They love it. Who wouldn't?" he says. Therefore, in a sustainable organisation, the concept of "wage" needs to be replaced by the concept of a "reward" that is fair, adjusted to performance, the capacity of the organisation and that can be proven by metrics.

We have developed five "equations" to demonstrate the usefulness of the elements we have chosen as key in the implementation of a fair rewarding system that will be embedded in the text that follows.

A SUSTAINABLE SYSTEM

MERIT IS A PRODUCT OF KNOWLEDGE AND TRANSPARENCY

First, any strategy for the implementation of such a system needs to be based on the concept of metric and the so-called meritocracy. In "The Meritocracy Myth", Stephen J. McNamee and Robert K. Miller state that merit is not a myth, but rather that the idea that "societal resources are distributed exclusively or primarily on the basis of individual merit is a myth".

However, to make a society or organisation more meritocratic, they suggest the reduction or elimination of all forms of discrimination, encouraging the wealthy to redistribute greater amounts of their accumulated wealth through philanthropy, a redesign of the tax system to become more progressive and the allocation of more government resources to provide equal access to critical services.

In a sustainable organisation that instils meritocracy, employees and executives will be rewarded for their contribution instead of simply receiving wages for the completion of a task, following the implementation of four key drivers: transparency, knowledge & influence, respect and commitment, that will enable the replacement of the concept of wage by the concept of a fair rewarding.

TRUST RESULTS FROM MERIT AND ACCOUNTABILITY

Secondly, the implementation of a meritocratic system necessarily has to go through a higher focus on transparency and accountability. This can be promoted within the organisation and through the implementation of adequate metrics so that it can be more easily assured that all employees and executives are compensated according to the effort and dedication they invest in the organisation. With these adequate metrics, namely the use of the median to calculate the CEO-to-worker ratio, organisations can be able to foster accountability and increase transparency, making rewards public among all members of the team and in the case of public companies, to the general public.

There are several cases of firms that have tried to instil further transparency. The technology giant Apple has been much discussed as it shows an ambiguous implementation of a policy of transparency. The firm has been called "the world's most secretive company"[198] and gained a bad reputation as a corporate citizen, due to scandals like the hoard of cash reserves, philanthropic missteps and an alliance with a high-profile electronics company which has been on the papers for poor working conditions, worker riots and a series of employee suicides.

However, according to Don Tapscott's *The Digital Economy*[199], this is another example that proves that transparency and the sharing of intellectual property can pay off. He argued that Apple had become more open in a number of areas and more transparent than one might think. Obviously, it is secretive regarding product announcements, not leaking any information to its customers, but also its employees. However, it shows a great deal of transparency and visibility when it comes to its supply chain and its owners.

Still, Tapscott believes Apple has failed miserably when it comes to the global community: although Apple has provided lower-cost computers to schools and universities, this has been seen as a mere marketing strategy and something that has little impact in the US' educational system. Due to the intense competitive pressures and scrutiny the company has been subjected to, Tapscott believes it will become an even more open company in the near future.

TRUST AND FAIRNESS DEVELOP HARMONY

While the implementation of the meritocratic system instils further transparency and also creates trust, it leads to a stronger sentiment of fairness. In other words, if an organisation is transparent about its practices, it will be easier for the employees and executives to trust the organisation. Ultimately, it will be possible to say that the organisation provides a fair treatment to its team. These elements can combine to bring harmony to organisation or the situation where there is agreement, concord, going back to the original definition of harmony. This enables the team and the organisation itself to fit together.

MERIT AND HARMONY PROMOTE MOBILISATION

Similarly, an agreement between the organisation and its team, together with a system where the team evolves through merit, can create further mobilisation. In other words, the act of assembling towards a common purpose.

A stronger focus on merit and the implementation of metrics that assure transparency will facilitate the implementation of rewards and the assurance that all the members of the team receive a fair compensation for their performance. Through transparency, employees can acknowledge the fairness of this compensation and enjoy more harmony among the team, which will necessarily lead to a stronger mobilisation – more organisation, preparedness for action, rallying for a common purpose – so that the whole team truly commits to achieve the organisation's goals and objectives.

STRATEGY, MERIT AND HARMONY CREATE SUSTAINABILITY!

If an organisation can successfully implement all of these elements, it will be closer to attaining sustainability, through a strategy embodied in the use of adequate metrics that assure a fair reward that is based on individual talent – merit – which is measured through examination and/or demonstrated achievement. In connection with the elements previously discussed, we can see how these steps are interlinked, as all of these elements take us back to the concept of respect and recognition discussed in the first point.

Therefore, through the implementation of transparency and the reinforcement of merit, employees can gain more **knowledge** in terms of the compensation practices of the organisation, which will in turn enable them to gain more **influence** over the employees.

SUSTAINABILITY EMPOWERS JUSTICE, SECURITY AND ULTIMATELY, HAPPINESS

Finally, together with the implementation of transparency, meritocracy and harmony comes balance. Altogether, these concepts will facilitate that assurance that a firm can remain sustainable and, more importantly, that its team will feel they are treated with justice, they have security in their professional life and last but not least, that they lead a happy life, the ultimate goal of this focus on sustainability.

With compensation practices characterised by transparency, accountability, a strong focus on merit and the provision of knowledge to the team, executives will consequently be more respected by the team, as it will feel they receive the necessary information to justify the reward they receive from their work. This will necessarily lead to more commitment by the team as it feels it has the necessary knowledge of the organisation's practices to feel committed to attaining collective goals and objectives.

Again, using the analogy of an orchestra, it is no good if the orchestra receives a whopping compensation for a performance if it does not receive the recognition, motivation and respect that go along with it. These are the necessary elements to ensure the orchestra's continued success. Similarly, in a sustainable organisation, these are also the elements that go hand in hand with security, opportunity and harmony, which come as crucial for the wellbeing of the community. However, the main difference is that the focus on cooperation is bound to create a communal effort to "stay at the top", while individuality does not lead to motivation within the rest of the community.

Here, in the same way as the maestro can decide to innovate the performance of his orchestra – but can only do so with the coordinated effort of the musicians – the CEO will need to become an agent of effective change. And in the same way that the maestro needs to motivate his musicians to achieve success, the CEO necessarily needs to be inspiring and adopt the aforementioned perspective of "courting to win".

THE COXSWAIN CEO

For the purpose of this chapter, we describe the general current practice as exaggerated in terms of executive compensation. This is because it still seems to be strongly linked to stock performance, rather than the performance of the executives themselves. Additionally, the tiers below the CEO receive a compensation that is not deemed as fair across the world and which seriously affects commitment, mobilisation and finally, happiness. In our opinion, this practice is not sustainable, as it goes against the principle of retaining talents and putting together a team that will work in a coordinated manner to achieve a common goal.

Therefore, in a sustainable organisation, we propose the analogy of a rowing crew against the passengers of a bus. The first represent a sustainable approach and the latter represent the common practices of the Old Economy. In the rowing crew, people use their individual strengths and everyone works together to achieve a common goal. The crew must row in a coordinated manner in the same direction, in order to get where they need to be and there are particular seats that need a stronger performance. In this case, the CEO would be the coxswain, the member of the crew who sits in the boat facing the bow, steers the boat and coordinates the power and rhythm of the rowers by communicating with the crew. The coxswain is the member of the team that encourages the rowers, the one they look up for motivation.

This is another example of a sustainable approach: the members of the crew get recognition according to their performance, but there is a sense of harmony among the team because all the members are equally important to achieve that goal. This context makes it easier to achieve the final goal – happiness – as all the conditions have been created for the team members to feel motivated, committed and fairly rewarded. Similarly, and using the analogy of the rowing boat, through these performance-based incentives, a company can assure that everyone in the rowing crew understands where they are trying to go and how to get there. Therefore, an incentive can be a powerful tool to motivate the team and reach a goal.

IMPLEMENTING A FAIRER RATIO

The major issue in implementing this step is the fact that it cannot possibly be ascertained, and that is where regulation comes as an essential tool. Here, we believe this can be successfully done in terms of CEO compensation and we are fierce advocates of the much-debated CEO-to-worker ratio. However, and as noted in the previous chapter, the use of the average to calculate the ratio will bring little value to the result, and that is why the median should be used instead, to better prevent outliers.

Therefore, for the sake of a fair reward, we propose the use of a ratio between 12:1 and 25:1, along the lines of what was proposed by Drucker, who saw this threshold as the one "beyond which they [the CEOs] cannot go if they don't want resentment and falling morale to hit their companies".

The reasoning behind this proposal has already been explained in the previous chapter and applies to many factors. There is, of course, the factor of justice. This is about assuring a ratio that controls any extreme discrepancies that lead to further inequality, the issue of valuing people for their work and not considering them as mere "passengers on the bus". Additionally, to take into account the theory of the "Marginal Million" – the distribution of a surplus million that can have a significant impact when compared to the impact it may have in the hands of the first holder. Then, there is the obvious factor of macro-economic development: with the extension of the market, and social recognition, the average class can see its quality of living highly improve.

Looking at the following graph, it is clear how a fair rewarding would impact the life and aims of an individual – which can be expanded to encompass the whole community.

Please note that this information is not by any means scientific. Rather, it is based on our research and on figures we consider to be reasonable across the developed world, which would obviously change when considered as one country alone, as the spending requirements will vary among countries.

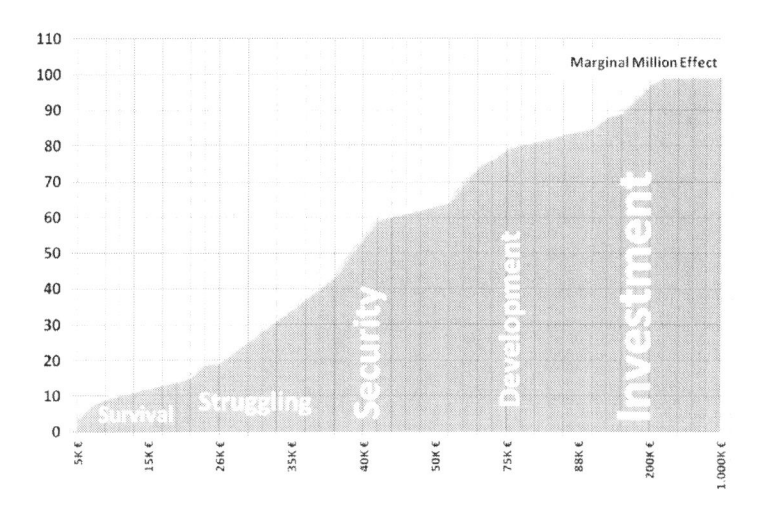

Fig. 4 – The impact that income can have on the level of happiness.

Thus, this is to be taken as a reference, a sort of benchmark where we want the figures to be merely indicative.

With 5,000 USD per year, one can only aim to **Survive**. That is to say, the income gained becomes mere means of subsistence, a means to survive. At this level, an individual will solely focus on his/her basic needs, which he/she will struggle to accomplish.

From the next level, starting at 20,000 USD per year, one will **Struggle** to accomplish his needs and wants. In other words, although an individual at this level will be able to survive, he/she will find it challenging to channel his/her earnings into his "want" rather than solely his "needs".

Moving up, we find a phase of **Security**, starting at 35,000 USD. This is where the individual has the means to survive, to provide a response to his/her and the family's needs and to think ahead, saving for his/her "wants" and for anything that may come unexpected, but this does not necessarily give the individual the means to think ahead and successfully save for his/her goals and objectives.

On the next level, which we have named **Development**, an individual can invest in education and create a higher potential for his/her family, travel, purchase goods, etc. It is only when an individual knows that he/she has the necessary income to survive, pay for any immediate needs and plan for potential needs, purchase goods, spend on entertainment and invest in the family's education and wellbeing that it is possible to move on to the top level – **Investment**.

At the **Investment** level, it is viable to take risks and think at a wider scale, by investing in the economy, creating projects and taking risks knowing that losing won't have an impact on the individual and his/her family's wellbeing and plans for the future.

The rationale of this analysis is that the Old Economy is characterised by a sense of imbalance. With the implementation of a balanced economy where workers obtain fair rewards and high discrepancies are controlled using common sense, harmony can be achieved, and as an obvious consequence, justice and security.

"To be neutral in a situation of injustice is to have chosen sides already. It is to support the status quo". – Desmond Tutu

Similar to the previous points, we have chosen a set of keywords throughout this point that illustrate a sustainable organisation in the shift from "Unfair wages to fair rewarding". Therefore, together with the implementation of the drivers mentioned above – transparency, knowledge & influence, respect and commitment, the aim is to implement the following shifts:

OLD ECONOMY		*SUSTAINABLE ORGANISATION*	
Average	The compensations within a firm are calculated using the average, which provides a weak reflection of the discrepancies between employees and top management.	Median	The use of the median enables the detection of outliers, providing a better reflection of inequality within a firm's compensation practices.
Survival	Employees work for survival and they envisage their work as the means to achieve a goal – salary. In terms of their outtake on life, work does not have a place in terms of contempt and satisfaction.	Harmony	Work is a means of achieving a harmonious living, through the satisfaction obtained with the goals achieved and the harmony achieved with a healthy environment at work.
Passive involvement	The employees are mere "passengers on the bus", without any active involvement and no authority on the projects assigned to them.	Full mobilisation	The employees coordinate and exchange roles and responsibilities for the sake of the result of the project; responsibilities are shared, and so is the participation.

OLD ECONOMY		SUSTAINABLE ORGANISATION	
Wage	The salary as per the contract signed with the employer; a fixed amount earned at the end of each month.	Reward	A compensation for the work performed – an incentive – that varies depending on the commitment of the employee, but which provides extra motivation.
Unlimited compensation	CEOs earn unlimited compensation, regardless of the performance of the company and the investment in the company itself and its employees.	CEO-to-worker ratio	The ratio controls the discrepancies between the CEO pay and the employee compensation to detect any extreme practices.
Work for money	Again, work is a means of getting paid – a necessary activity for survival.	Work to stay at the top	Work is a means of achieving goals and gaining personal – and collective – satisfaction and a sense of achievement.
Star Athlete	CEOs are seen as star athletes, the so-called Super Managers that represent the company and are responsible for the whole performance of the company.	Courting to win	The CEOs are examples to follow, charismatic, and succeed in motivating and encouraging the employees to undertake a collective effort towards short and long-term objectives.

The set of words on the left describes the practices based on imbalanced wages and unlimited compensations for top management, which foster inequality across economies and strengthen the image of the CEO as a super athlete, although the performance of the company is not necessarily tied to a specific action by the CEO. The set of the words on the right represents the compensation practice of the new economy, focused on fair rewarding, based on incentives, pay-for-performance and encouraging practices that provide employees with further motivation, and the CEO of the new economy. The CEO takes a fair pay for the wellbeing of the organisation and the economy and shares the success of the company with his/her team.

4 – FROM STOCK PERFORMANCE TO THE SUSTAINABLE ORGANISATION INDEX

"The world is still very vulnerable to bubbles". – Robert Schiller, American economist and academic

"Speculation is only a word covering the making of money out of the manipulation of prices, instead of supplying goods and services". – Henry Ford, American industrialist

"Another great evil arising from this desire to be thought rich; or rather, from the desire not to be thought poor, is the destructive thing which has been honoured by the name of speculation; but which ought to be called Gambling." – William Cobbett, English pamphleteer, farmer and journalist

"I'd be a bum on the street with a tin cup if the markets were efficient". – Warren Buffett, American business magnate

"Volatility is a symptom that people have no idea of the underlying value". – Jeremy Grantham, British investor

"The stock market is filled with individuals who know the price of everything, but the value of nothing". – Phillip Fisher, American stock investor

"In the financial world, it tends to be misleading to state 'There is no free lunch'. Rather, the more meaningful comment is: 'Somebody has to pay for lunch'". – Martin Whitman, American investment advisor

"Price is what you pay. Value is what you get". — Charlie Munger, American business magnate

"Money won't create success, the freedom to make it will." — Nelson Mandela

"Speculation" has been the buzzword of the century when it comes to discussing the economy. Speculators, described by a paper[200] published by Wharton Digital Press, University of Pennsylvania, represent "someone who tries to profit from an asset by anticipating how its price will change either by buying it in expectation that the price will rise, or selling short in anticipation that the price will fall". The paper adds that speculators tend to focus on the short-term and may be willing to take on more risk than typical investors.

As a result, "speculation has become a sort of a derogatory term to describe investors who are acting recklessly", says Bernard Baumohol, chief global economist at the Princeton-based Economic Outlook Group. "I think that it is unfortunate because they do contribute to the market", he adds. Baumohl believes that speculators may be less interested in the actual value of an asset and more interested in the emotions that drive the market. "I have a sense that speculators spend more time trying to understand the short-term psychology that affects trade than the underlying value of how something might perform", he explains further, giving the example of the dot-com bubble in the 1990s, when investors poured money into Internet start-ups that had not made a profit.

DOES SPECULATION BRING ANY ECONOMIC BENEFIT?

In much the same way that speculation has been long associated with manipulation to achieve certain results, be it the abuse of power, disconnection from a real value (and rather on a virtual and volatile value) or even corruption, it is also criticised as being used as a scapegoat, Professor Craig Pirrong explains. The

Finance and Energy Markets professor at the Bauer College of Business believes that some movements likened to speculation, like commodity prices, are based on fundamentals, more than speculation. He even talks about "bad speculation", where manipulation tries to corner markets by buying so much of a commodity that the price soars to a high.

Although the recently-passed Dodd-Frank Act contains provisions to counter speculation, its results remain doubtful, Pirrong adds. "Generally, I'm very sceptical that there is any constructive policy that would serve to whittle out the bad speculation from the good speculation", he says. The best way to address manipulation, he explains, "is by imposing penalties on manipulators after the fact – rather than by indiscriminate restrictions on the actions of market participants, virtually none of whom are manipulating or even can manipulate".

However, despite the view that speculators cause price volatility, they often stabilise prices or bring them closer to what they should be, Wharton Professor Jeremy Siegel explains. Although he believes that regulators should enforce rules against illegal trading practices and maintain marginal requirements to assure that speculators gamble mostly with their own money, he thinks that banning speculation would create more problems than it would solve. "History has generally concluded that although speculators may occasionally send the price of an asset too high or too low, on balance, speculators increase the amount of information in the market".

Furthermore, in a paper entitled *Executive Compensation and Short-Termist Behaviour in Speculative Markets*[201], published by the National Bureau of Economic Research (NBER), Bolton, Sheinkman and Wong state that rent-seeking CEOs are encouraged to pursue short-term speculative projects. This comes at the expense of long-term fundamental value due to the nature of the link between the firm's performance and the movements in the stock market. They propose a series of solutions, namely the reform of the current structure of CEO pay (in the US), which calls for a regulatory response to strengthen boards of directors, as well as audit and remuneration committees. Similarly, the authors propose limits on CEOs' ability to unwind their own stock holdings in short horizons, which could provide a more effective deterrent to the pursuit of short-term strategies.

The use of money in manipulation and control practices is tightly connected to speculation and corruption and this makes it clear that these practices cannot be associated with sustainability. Rather, sustainability can be achieved when organisations aim to be measured by their capacity to create value, instead of focusing on the virtual and unforeseeable movement of the stock market. This happens because the stock market is subject to a high volatility, intense speculation and debatable measures like high-speed trading, even if this has not been implemented across the corporate world.

Due to the aforementioned facts, markets are no longer considered as liquidity mechanisms for organisations and tend to work more like betting houses, where groups control the results, thus controlling the performance of the organisations (the original indicator of stock movement) and ultimately controlling the salaries of top management.

Moreover, it is our belief that markets have become inefficient because they are controlled in the hands of a few institutions, especially as practices like high-speed trading are still legally allowed. As well as this, they have become inefficient due to a lack of competition in most markets, and in several markets, like financial markets, the people who take the decisions are not the ones who own the capital.

A CHANGE OF PURPOSE

The fact that the vast majority of organisations are valued by their stock market value and not by the actual value that they produce is one of the factors that would necessarily have to change to turn any organisation sustainable, so this value does not remain a concept that can be negotiated.

However, over the last century, measurement systems and the focus on stock market profits and shareholder value has remained the same and the way measurements are performed defines the results we may expect. For example, a football team can play fantastically well, but can still be defeated if the other team scores more goals. Also, while rugby has control systems in place to supervise the match using TV technology, this degree of transparency is not used in football, which provides more leeway for mistakes.

A sustainable organisation needs to be seen as a community formed by people with two main goals: providing a product and/or a service and creating their own subsistence. Using the analogy of the orchestra, this would happen much the same way as the members of an orchestra choose to become musicians to gain a living but need to pursue constant improvement opportunities and cannot rely on volatile factors to move up in their careers.

For this to happen, the community would have to be fully involved. This can be done through the process of stakeholder engagement whereby an organisation involves people who may be affected by the decisions it makes or who can influence the implementation of the decisions. This community can then support or oppose the decisions, is influential in the organisation or within the community.

The underlying principle in this stakeholder engagement is that stakeholders have the chance to influence the decision-making process, which differentiates stakeholder engagement from communication process that seeks to issue a message or influence groups to agree with a decision that is already made. The biggest benefit from this process is that it provides the opportunity to align business practices further with societal needs and expectations, helping to drive long-term sustainability.

This is also a key part of Corporate Social Responsibility (CSR) and achieving the "triple bottom line" (TBL), an accounting framework that considers the three Ps: people, planet and profit – the so-called "three pillars of sustainability". Many organisations have adopted this framework to evaluate their performance in a broader context and while in traditional business accounting, the bottom line refers to "profit" or "loss", which is usually recorded at the bottom line of a statement of revenue and expenses, this broader definition introduces the concept of full cost accounting. For example, if an organisation shows monetary profit, but their asbestos mine causes thousands of deaths from asbestosis, the triple bottom line will add two more bottom lines – social and environmental. Although the TBL brings some challenges, like finding applicable data and determining how a project contributes towards sustainability, it is still fairly efficient when it comes to enabling organisations to take a long-term perspective and evaluate the future consequences of certain decisions.

Similarly, Greenberg's[202] concept of organisational justice is another measure that can be used to increase owners' engagement in impact measurement. The concept is based on how an employee judges the behaviour of the organisation and the employees' resulting attitude and behaviour, with the principle that individuals react to actions and decisions made by organisations every day and that the individuals' perceptions of these decisions as fair or unfair can influence their attitudes and behaviours.

The idea of organisational justice stems from the equity theory (Adams) which states that judgements of equity and inequity derive from comparisons between one's self and others based on inputs and outcomes. The outcome of this organisational justice will be affected by employees' perceptions and common outcomes will include trust, performance, job satisfaction, organisational commitment, organisational citizenship behaviours, counterproductive work behaviours, absenteeism, turnover and emotional exhaustion.

TRUE VALUE

Based on the principle that an assessment based on speculation is highly damaging for the sustainability of any organisation, we believe the ultimate goal for an organisation seeking to become sustainable should be to create real value. In other words, to achieve a situation where the products and/or services provided by a given organisation have a real impact on the market and the communities where the organisation operates.

This concept goes along the lines of the concept of Shared Value[203]. According to Michael E. Porter and Mark R. Kramer, the authors of the article entitled *Creating Shared Value*, "a big part of the problem lies with companies themselves, which remain trapped in an outdated approach to value creation that has emerged over the past few decades. They continue to view value creation narrowly, optimising short-term financial performance in a bubble while missing the most important customer needs and ignoring the broader influences that determine their longer-term success".

The authors believe that, "companies must take the lead in bringing business and society back together" through the principle of shared value, "which involves creating economic value in a way that also creates value for society by addressing its needs and challenges". They recognise this as a way to achieve "economic success" and which could give rise to "the next major transformation of business thinking".

This way, organisations can set policies and practices thinking not just about the organisation at an internal level, but also about the economy as a whole, particularly in the community where the organisation operates. This is based on the belief that the assessment of value based on stock performance is not indicative of the performance of the leader of the organisation. Rather, sustainable organisations should be assessed by their capacity to create value, encouraging the presence of highly skilled leaders that can truly push the organisation's performance up.

Keeping to our analogy of the organisation as an orchestra and the leader as the conductor, the maestro does not earn his salary from merely showing up at a concert, but rather through a consolidated performance that has given rise to certain expectations. In the same way that a good maestro cannot accommodate to a past performance that represented a good effort, a good leader should not be able to do this either. Finally, orchestra musicians would need to receive equal treatment, strongly focused on captivation through the figure of the leader, so that the organisation can achieve a sense of community and a set of values that will enable the consolidation of the ultimate goal – achieving sustainability.

Owners < (Team + Community)

In a sustainable organisation, value directed to the owners is always inferior to the sum of the value directed to the team and the value directed to the community. Obviously, to perform this calculation, organisations would have to be capable of fully assessing the internal and external impact they have on the market and the communities where they operate and replace an inwards-focusing practice by a more outwards approach where the employees, the community and the society as a whole are part of the strategy of the organisation.

Through this internal and external outlook, the organisation can develop usefulness and meaning in the way it pursues its purpose without having to follow the unforeseeable movement of the stock market. In the same way as the organisation's goals and objectives are focused on a wider audience – the society as a whole – and show respect and care for their members, the community and the society, they also become more meaningful to this society, which feels that it is truly part of the organisation's strategy.

Consequently, the organisation is able to gain an approach that is not so much focused on speculation but rather on accountability, predictability and other measurable factors. Altogether, these elements can foster sustainability in the way that the company can adopt a strategy that can be easily implemented and transferable across the corporate world and the economy.

Furthermore, without a sense of captivation – what we call 'courting' – allied to a sense of communities and a proper set of values (as defined in the previous proposals), no sustainability can be achieved.

THE SUSTAINABLE ORGANISATION INDEX (SORG)

Over the last century, despite all changes, the measurement system and the focus of organisations have remained highly concentrated on profits and shareholder value. This has highly influenced people's perspective of value as the way that any organisation performs these measurements defines the very results that may be expected.

Our aim is to create a new sustainability indicator – the Sustainable Organisation Index (SORG). Like any index, "it is something that helps you understand where you are, which way you are going and how far you are from where you want to be", Sustainable Measures explains.[204] Furthermore, it becomes increasingly important as it helps any organisation receive an alert to a problem before it gets too bad and obviously, it helps the organisation progress through a better-positioned indicator.

In the case of a sustainable economy, an indicator would focus on areas where there are weak links between the economy, the environment and the society. In the case of organisations, we will focus on the link between the owners of the company, the people working for the company (employees, or the team) and the people affected by the company (the community).

Again, using the example of a traditional indicator, the GDP, which measures the monetary value of all the finished goods and services produced within a country's borders in a specific period, the higher the indicator, the better the economic wellbeing is assumed to be. When it comes to the SORG, the higher the indicator, the higher the balance between the owners, employees and the community and the higher the value distributed among them.

As mentioned in the first chapter, the problem with the GDP is that it only reflects the amount of economic activity, regardless of the effect of that activity on the community. That is precisely what the SORG wants to avoid. To that effect, it provides a more comprehensive picture of organisational progress, environmental impact and the balance in terms of value distribution among the employees. In essence, it is a bit similar to the Index of Sustainable Economic Welfare (ISEW), with the difference that it focuses on organisations and not the economy as a whole. We believe that, by measuring organisations, the impact at the economic level will be a direct consequence.

In our hypothesis, an organisation is just a group of people, gathered around a common purpose, to serve the community and it is sustainable if there is a balanced distribution of economic flow among the owners, the team (employees) and the community. The direct value of the organisation's activity is measured by its revenue and the positive or negative impact it may generate over time - after all, it represents the value the community assigns to the organisation's product(s) or service(s).

Our main challenge is to compare organisations transparently regardless of their size, industry and purpose, using only data available to the public. This is the purpose of the SORG. In the cases presented, what we want to show is not a definite solution, but rather a possible approach using the limited information available. Our challenge has been to make sense of this limited information and our hope is that this will show how further transparency could bring significant results by making this information fully available to everyone.

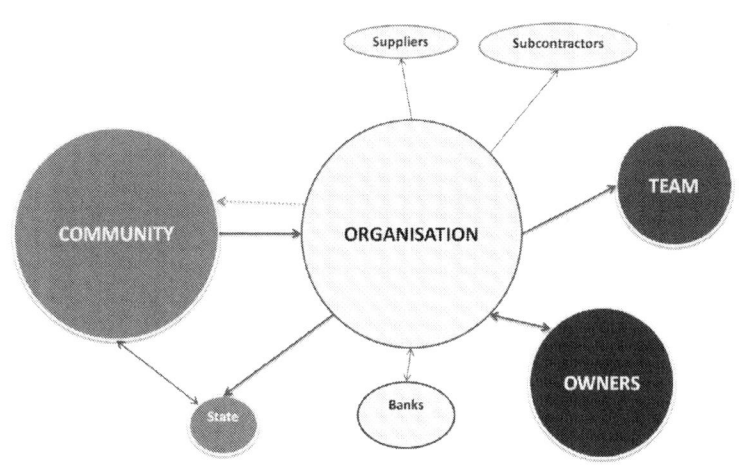

Fig.5 – The Organisation relationship model

The diagram above illustrates the economic flows between the organisation and the internal and external groups that affect it: revenues, salaries, interests, costs, taxes and dividends (blue lines). In the case of non-profit organisations with no revenues, the flow comes from the organisation to the community in the form of donations or voluntary work (green line).

In our hypothesis, we assume that organisations can only be sustainable if there is a balance between COMMUNITY, TEAM and OWNERS.

So in a sustainable organisation C+T ≥ O and C ≥ T. Additionally, as we mentioned in the previous chapter, in a sustainable organisation, the distribution of all salaries should follow a bell-shaped normal curve and the highest-to-median salary ratio should be lower[205] than 12 to guarantee harmony among all members.

COMMUNITY, TEAM and OWNERS are defined by (all the data is taken from financial reports available online):

COMMUNITY = REVENUES - COGS - INTEREST + TAXES + IMPACT

Revenues represent the value recognised by the community impacted by the organisation's activity. COGS is the cost of goods sold (suppliers and subcontractors). We deduct the cogs and interest (banks) because that flow goes to external organisations to the one under analysis. Taxes are added since taxes are flows that theoretically return to the community.

Impact is the positive or negative consequence of the organisation's activity over time. It's an important indicator associated with each industry, activity. Impact should be a factor determined in function of revenues. In a form:

$$I(r) = \sum_{i=1}^{n} Fi \times r$$

Where I is the Impact, r are the revenues, F are the factors for each of the n criteria affected by the organisation activity.

As a wrap-up to this chapter, we propose an example of a model considering the environmental, health, security and development criteria to determine the impact of any activity/industry.

$TEAM = T_{EAM} S_{ALARY} + A_{LL} B_{ENEFITS}$

TEAM represents the sum of employee salaries. It should include any type of equity compensation (benefits).

$O_{WNERS} = N_{ET} I_{NCOME} - TEQUITY$

TEQUITY is the proportion of net income owned by the team. We consider team ownership in TEAM, so it must be deducted here. Some members of the organisation may have two roles, as TEAM and OWNERS. When this happens we include all the flow in TEAM. However, TEQUITY is not always publicly available.

Now to analyse the distribution of the flow between these three entities, for one fiscal year, we use the following ratios.

$$SORG\ I = \frac{COMMUNITY}{OWNERS}$$

The SORGI (Sustainable Organisation Index I) measures the balance between the owners of the organisation in the community. The higher the value, the higher the benefits the community gets. It only applies when net income is positive. In a sustainable organisation SORGI ≥ 1

$$SORG\ II = \frac{TEAM \times HARMONY}{OWNERS}$$

The SORGII (Sustainable Organisation Index II) measures the internal balance of the organisation. The higher the number, the better and it only applies when net income is positive. Harmony measures fairness. It is given by:

$$HARMONY = \frac{TEAM\ MEDIAN^2}{TEAM\ AVERAGE \times CEO}$$

The TEAM MEDIAN and TEAM AVERAGE are the average and median of the salaries and benefits from all people that work in the organisation. The CEO represents the total salary and benefits of the highest salary in the organisation, normally the CEO. The HARMONY index measures internal cohesion. In a sustainable organisation, harmony is always greater than 1. The higher the index, the better.

$$SORG\ III = \frac{COMMUNITY}{TEAM}$$

The SORGIII (Sustainable Organisation Index III) measures balance between the TEAM of the organisation in the COMMUNITY. The higher the value, the higher the benefits the community gets. In a sustainable organisation, SORGIII ≥ 1

To assess how balanced the organisation is, both at an internal and external level, we use the following formula:

$$SORG = \frac{COMMUNITY^2 \times TEAM\ MEDIAN^2}{OWNERS^2 \times TEAM\ AVERAGE \times CEO}$$

The SORG (Sustainable Organisation Index) is a product of SORGI, SORGII and the SORGIII Index and indicates a cumulative effect. In a sustainable organisation SORG ≥ 1. In a multi-year analysis, which offers a more precise evaluation of the organisation's activities, each variable should be calculated by the sum of its values for all the fiscal years under analysis.

It is important to note that this can be calculated using only public data but more accurate results could be assured if organisations made salaries publicly available and the IMPACT factor known. Still, it is useful to assess any organisation regardless of its size, industry or purpose.

Overall, the SORG comes as a valuable tool to acquire a clear image of how the organisation behaves in the society and whether or not it is free from speculation, based on factual information publicly available: it is very simple to calculate and it offers a transparent assessment of the sustainability of any organisation.

APPLYING THE SORG

To illustrate the application of SORG in 4 completely different types of organisations, considering the data on the table below, we calculated the SORGI, SORGII, Harmony and SORG indexes for MacDonald's, Boeing, Google and Wikipedia.

Company	Market Cap	Revenue	Employees	Net Income	Cost Of Goods Sold	Taxes	Interest	Average Salary (USD per year)	Median salary (USD per year)	CEO x MEDIAN
MacDonald's	89,04	28,11	440.000	5,59	11,19	2,6200	0,52150	20.000	22.000	434,53
Boeing	87,05	86,62	168.400	4,58	73,190	1,6500	0,4610	75.000	79.300	198,00
Wikipedia		44.667	208	12930	19.721			76.846	76.846	1,00
Google	346,3	59,73	55.030	12,21	25,820	2,2800	0,08300	70.000	115.900	1,00

Note: Market Capitalization, Revenues, Net Income, COGS, Taxes and Interest are in Billions, excepting for Wikipedia that is in Thousands

Fig. 6. Company data

All financial data was collected from Wolfram Alpha (2013 filing data), median salaries from PayScale.com Dec 2014, average salaries from Careerbliss.com and Wikipedia data from Wikipedia's financial report 2013. <u>Wikipedia revenue, cogs and net income are in thousands</u>. TEAM was calculated using average salaries x employees. For these examples, we did not find information about TEQUITY, so TEQUITY was considered zero. In these analyses, we did not consider the IMPACT factor, since it is not yet available.

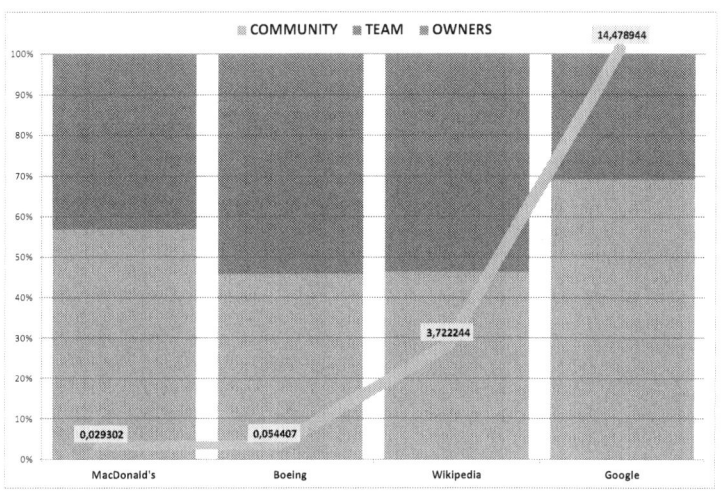

Fig. 7 – Applying the SORG

This graph synthesises sustainability of any type of organisation. We overlap graphs of different scales just to offer a simplified analysis.

At first glance — using a colour graph where green represent community, blue represent team and red represent owners – we get the impact of the colours in the background graph. In this case the difference in colours is evident. The colours represent the proportion between COMMUNITY, TEAM and OWNERS. The bigger the green area, the better and the opposite goes for the red area. In a sustainable organisation, considering our hypotheses, BLUE+GREEN ≥ RED. As we can see from this example, MacDonald's clearly does not benefit the community. Boeing and Wikipedia look balanced and Google clearly benefits the community.

Looking at the SORG Index line, we can see that Google's sustainability index is 494 times higher than MacDonald's ... and only 5 times higher than Wikipedia's. The difference in this example is so big that the line had to be skewed to fit both extreme points in the graph.

Now, why are Google and Wikipedia's SORG so high? Because those organisations, besides providing clear benefits to the community and a high leverage owners' effect, have an outstanding internal cohesion, which probably explains our first observation and the results presented by those organisations.

GOING DEEPER IN THE ANALYSIS: BREAKING UP SORG

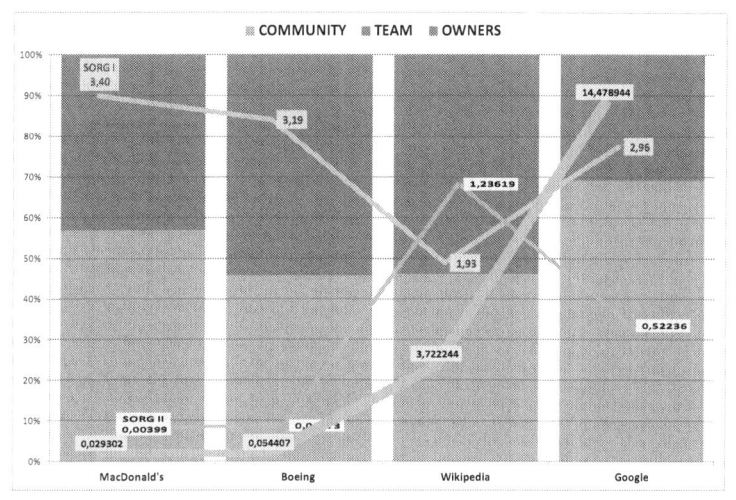

Fig. 8. Breaking up the SORG between the team, the community and the owners

Looking in more detail, we can further explain our first analysis by separating the external and internal impact of the owners' leverage – SORGI and SORGII. Again, each line uses a different scale but we overlap it just to offer a simplified analysis.

We observe the consistency of Wikipedia and Google and even MacDonald's. Boeing's inconsistency is due essentially to the HARMONY factor. That can be explained looking at the CEO-to-median salary ratio (see Company Table on "Applying the SORG"). The harmony and cohesion champion is clearly Wikipedia.

This analysis is thus useful to explain the behaviour of the SORG Index further.

*It is important to note that this data did not consider the impact factor. Empirically, we know that if we had considered the impact factor, the results would be even more emphasised but with the same trend.

GOING DEEPER IN THE ANALYSIS: LOOKING INSIDE THE ORGANISATION

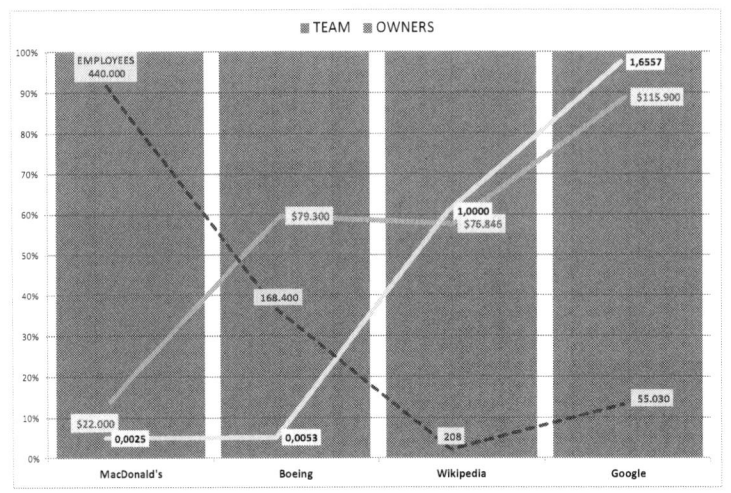

Fig.9. Internal assessment

Here, we can see the Harmony Index that so strongly influenced SORGII. It is easily explained by the distribution of the salaries and the CEO-to-median salary ratio. Besides, we clearly see that, despite having a USD 22,000 median, the TEAM factor in MacDonald's is high because of the organisation's 440,000 employees. This means that the TEAM factor is obviously influenced by the size of the organisation, even if the salaries are low. This makes sense because, even distributing low salaries, the organisation has a big impact in the society.

The "blue" factor in Google, associated with its harmony factor, means that the organisation generates a high income per employee. It is known that an organisation like Google has a strong Employee Ownership and this may be one of the reasons behind such a high proportion directed towards owners.

CONCLUDING THE SORG ANALYSIS

Observing these three graphs, it is easy to understand how the value generated by the organisation is distributed among the COMMUNITY, the TEAM and the OWNERS. In this example, it becomes clear how much the HARMONY factors affects both Boeing and MacDonald's and how unbalanced MacDonald's seems to be. On the other hand, it also becomes evident that Google and Wikipedia are balanced in the way they benefit the COMMUNITY. If the IMPACT factor was known, the trend would be accentuated: more unbalance to MacDonald's and Boeing and more balance to Google and Wikipedia.

This analysis becomes especially interesting if these results are compared with the market capitalisation of these organisations, with the advantage of being immune to speculation. A wider analysis considering 5 or more years of the organisation's activities will provide a more accurate perspective of the organisation's sustainability.

THE IMPACT FACTOR

As noted in the definition of Community, the IMPACT factor is considered strongly relevant. Unfortunately, we did not find a universal and normalised analysis of impact by industry or activity. In our perspective, to truly and transparently analyse the real outcome of an organisation, it is extremely important to measure the result of the organisation's activity over time. Empirically, it is very easy to realise that some activities have a strongly negative impact, as is the case of oil & and gas, armament and fast food, while others can have a very positive leverage, like education, health and environment. So, the purpose of the Impact factor is to determine the net benefit of any activity over time.

As we defined previously, the IMPACT factor can be calculated by:

$$I(r) = \sum_{i=1}^{n} Fi \times r$$

Where I is the Impact, r are the revenues, F are the factors for each of n the criteria affected by the organisation's activity.

Taking the oil & gas industry as an example, the social cost of carbon is widely known and publicly available. According to data by the US government from May 2013 (Interagency Working Group on Social Cost of Carbon), the cost of cleaning 1 ton of CO2 is USD $221. Therefore, turning these calculations into something easy for everyone to understand, the cost of cleaning one barrel of oil is $95.03. We do not know what price oil is while you are reading this sentence. However, this will probably come as a surprise to you.

As an example to demonstrate the influence of IMPACT, running the SORG index on oil & gas major ExxonMobil and just taking into account the environmental criteria, we can show that the SORG goes from 2.12397 to -16.8853[206], which shows how deeply the impact factor can affect the sustainability of an organisation, which is obvious because someone will have to pay for the mess...

Company	Cap (bn USD)	Revenue (bn USD)	Employees	Income (bn USD)	Cost of goods sold	Taxes	Interest	Average Salary	Median Salary
ExxonMobil	421,7	436,5	75.000	5,82	284	22,03	0,066	$44.000	$96.900

Company	Impact	SORG
ExxonMobil	-667,90	-16,885

Fig.10. Impact table: Calculation with the impact and without the impact

Unfortunately, the environmental impact is never considered when analysing organisations and so we tend to be misguided by the real value of some organisations. Apparently, they generate a positive outcome when looking at the revenues, but when we go deeper, we see that their activity will negatively impact the environment for generations to come.

It is not fair that our taxes will be, at least partially, wasted on cleaning or recovering from the mess some industries generate. That has a price but unfortunately most people ignore it and the transgressors benefit from it.

As you can see, one of the critical points when calculating the impact is to use units that are directly comparable. Revenue is a factor common to any organisation (with the exception of non-profit organisations with no revenue).

The idea is very simple. Imagine that we could calculate the average profit someone would get from a USD $1,000 investment in education. It's not difficult to realise that, empirically, this profit will be several times those $1,000.

Taking another example, we can calculate the impact of an organisation like Médecins Sans Frontières (MSF) considering two main criteria: health – we could look at how much it would cost to treat someone with MSF, a positive impact measured in terms of the number of people treated – and development, because every healthy person will at least have the capability of generating a minimum amount of US dollars per year.

Looking at Walmart, we can analyse a different kind of impact on the community. According to a study undertaken by Americans for Tax Fairness, a coalition of 400 national and state-level progressive groups[207], published on April 15, 2014, the multinational retail corporation's workers are costing US taxpayers an estimated $6.2 billion in public assistance including food stamps, Medicaid and subsidised housing. The report found that "a single Walmart Supercenter cost taxpayers between $904,542 and $1.75 million per year, or between $3,015 and $5,815 on average for each of 300 workers".

A similar study showed that the American fast food industry outsourced a combined $7 billion in annual labour costs to taxpayers, accounting $1.2 billion of that total to MacDonald's alone.

Impact analysis can also be useful to value non-profit organisations. In the case of Wikipedia, for instance, it is estimated that it could be worth tens of billions of dollars, according to an article on Smithsonian Mag[208]. The blog and cooperative resource site hosted by the American University InfoJustice (www.infojustice.org), researchers Jonathan Band and Jonathan Gerafi identified a few factors that could help value an organisation like Wikipedia, namely market value, replacement cost and consumer value.

They reached this conclusion by looking at what other sites that get similar traffic are worth, how much people would be willing to pay for Wikipedia and how much would it cost to replace the site[209]. In the end, they concluded it is worth "tens of billions of dollars" with a replacement cost of $6.6 billion dollars. "The millions of hours contributed by volunteer writers and editors leverage this modest budget, funded by donations, into an asset worth tens of billions of dollars that produces hundreds of billions of dollars of consumer benefit", they wrote.

We could use the same rationale to calculate any impact from an activity through four criteria that are essential to human life: environment, health, security and development. Those are all the needs humans can aspire.

INDUSTRY	TYPE OF IMPACT			
	ECOLOGICAL	HEALTH	SECURITY	DEVELOPMENT
OIL IT'S EASY TO RELATE BARREL WITH REVENUES	- $96x Barrel THIS IS AN OFFICIAL VALUE	-0,2x Revenues		
JUNK FOOD		- 2x Revenues		
COMPUTERS	-0,5 Revenues			+2 x Revenues
LEARNING				+3 x Revenues
HUMANITARIAN NGO		+500xPeopleHelped		+100xPeopleHelped
ARMAMENT			- FxRevenues	

Fig. 11. Types of impact

These are merely simple ideas. What we aspire to achieve with this book is to inspire people, especially academics, to go deeper in this analysis and generate a full impact table that shows the real economic impact of any activity humans may develop. Such an impact table would be useful, not only for the purpose of supplementing this SORG analysis, but also as an additional framework to guide investment decisions.

EXTREME TYPES OF ORGANISATIONS

The application of the SORG index enables us to categorise organisations into different groups, according to the results. These groups determine whether the organisation is more focused on its TEAM, the OWNERS or the COMMUNITY.

"Prince John" Organisations:

Prince John was the sworn enemy of the 14th century legendary outlaw hero Robin Hood, who robbed and killed representatives of the authority to give the gains to the poor[210]. The character, based on the real life of King Richard of England, was shown to continuously find ways to rob and swindle his people in the pursuit of wealth. We use the "Prince John" designation to describe organisations where the revenue directed to the OWNERS by the organisation is superior to the revenue directed to the TEAM and the COMMUNITY, or $O \geq T+C$. In other words, organisations where the focus lies on the creation of wealth for the owners themselves at the cost of the workers and the community it affects. In this type of organisations, the SORG is always lower than 1.

"Robin Hood" Organisations:

These would be the exact opposite of Prince John organisations, where the organisation directs most of its revenue to the COMMUNITY, or $C \geq O+T$. These include organisations where the revenue is inevitably focused on the community it affects and not the workers or the owners. In this type of organisations, the SORG is always greater than 1.

"Brotherhoods":

Brotherhoods are commonly described as groups or organisations of people who share the same interests and jobs, characterised by feelings of friendship, support and understanding between people. In brotherhood organisations, the distribution of revenue widely favours the TEAM, rather than the community or the owners, or $T \geq C+O$. This group could include organisations like sport clubs, NGO and government entities, where the TEAM clearly use community and owners trust and passion to benefit disproportionally. In this type of organisation, the SORG is always lower than 1.

This is a very simple classification that may help any citizen to understand the real purpose of any given organisation. It could also prove extremely useful if integrated in the rankings for world top organisations.

(To comment the SORG index or to contribute to the development of the IMPACT analyses, get involved at: http//www.thesustainableorganisation.com)

Similarly to the previous points, we have chosen a set of keywords throughout this point that illustrate a sustainable organisation in the shift from "Market Cap Evaluation". Therefore, through the drivers mentioned above – Internal & external Impact; Usefulness, Meaning; Non-speculative; Sustainability the aim is to implement the following shifts:

OLD ECONOMY		SUSTAINABLE ORGANISATION	
Power	Each tier of the organisational structure has a higher level of power.	Merit	Different roles regard each other with respect, with an equal level of power.
Envy	Members of the organisation envy peers and top management for their working conditions and rewards.	Recognition Respect	Members of the organisation recognise peers and management merits
Competition	Employees compete to achieve better outcomes than their counterparts.	Cooperation	The members of the organisation cooperate to achieve a common goal.
Struggle	Employees struggle in jobs that give them no recognition of their value, or no adequate reward.	Harmony	The members of the organisation cooperate in harmony, due to the sense of equality instilled in the spirit of the organisation.
Obligation	Employees work out of obligation.	Captivation/ Courting	The members of the organisation are captivated by top management to cooperate better to achieve a common goal.
Stock performance	The performance of the organisation	Sustainable Organisation Index	The performance of the organisation is assessed as a result of

OLD ECONOMY			SUSTAINABLE ORGANISATION
	depends on the performance of the stock market.		the value it creates to its internal and external community (SORGI and SORGII).
Speculation	The performance of the company is controlled by a volatile market, ruled by speculation.	Well-defined accomplish-ments	The performance of the company is controlled by the accomplishment of well-defined goals and objectives.

CONCLUSION

"To me, business is not about wearing suits or pleasing stockholders. It is about being true to yourself, your ideas and focusing on the essentials". – Richard Branson

"Live as if you were to die tomorrow. Learn as if you were to live forever". – Mahatma Gandhi

"If you can't feed a hundred people, then feed just one". – Mother Teresa

"My role in society, or any artist's or poet's role, is to try and express what we all feel. Not to tell people how to feel. Not as a preacher, not as a leader, but as a reflection of us all". – John Lennon

"As we look ahead into the next century, leaders will be those who empower others". – Bill Gates

"Today knowledge has power. It controls access to opportunity and advancement". – Peter F. Drucker

Over the last decades, information technology has revolutionised the way people communicate and interact, creating a New Economy. The Internet has made information widely available and accessible and empowered curiosity and influence. Curious minds can now be limitless and free, regardless of their origin, age or gender. With this New Economy, the world has become smaller and more reachable. However, organisational models have largely stayed the same, maintaining assessment practices that are still highly based on speculative drivers.

It is common understanding that communication is at the heart of any organisation. So, why have organisational models not evolved accordingly? To truly leverage the potential of this information age, we need to rethink and redesign organisations. Today we know that the brightest moments of human development have been those when knowledge and communication expanded. In line with this thought, the New Economy brings the need to tap people's curiosity, quest for knowledge and understanding, in order to develop a sustainable society.

Yet, this sustainability does not survive on knowledge alone, but rather on shared knowledge that clarifies curiosity and empowers trust and transparency. Both of these are crucial elements in sustainable relationships. Knowing that organisations are at the core of our society, it then becomes clear that humanity needs these organisations to prosper. There, the creation of a transparent, accessible, dynamic and meritocratic organisation model can generate sustainable organisations and as a result, a sustainable society.

The sustainable organisation model hereby proposed, and the Sustainable Organisation Index (SORG), originates from our curiosity to understand the world we live in as well as an attempt to improve this world. We simply want people to understand, think, compare and make wise decisions, based on the premise that wisdom is the foundation of security and development. Founded on new values, relationships, metrics and purposes, this sustainable organisation model is our attempt to change the way that organisations are built and perceived by society.

The SORG index is a corollary of this new model. It is a simple and transparent tool that enables anyone to understand the real outcome of any organisation from the perspective of sustainability. Through the SORG, we believe that anyone can easily and freely understand the real outcome of any given organisation, regardless of its size, location or purpose, anywhere and at any time. This is still unique today!

With this book, we aspire to instil readers to start looking at organisations individually and the society in general, with a permanent curiosity, transparency and intelligence. As a transparent society is our major guarantee to security and development, we hope this will represent a decisive contribution to a fair and sustainable society built on sustainable organisations.

Thank you for reading!

Reader's comments, **ideas**, cases, suggestions and participation are Welcome!

http//www.thesustainableorganisation.com

ABOUT THE AUTHORS

Miguel Reynolds Brandão, is a father of 4. Curious and independent by nature, he is graduated in engineering and management. He is a serial entrepreneur who started his first venture in his early twenties. Today, he mostly works as a business strategist, negotiator, business broker and mentor. He has authored books and articles on strategic management systems, entrepreneurship, business brokering and teleworking and has participated in several international events in those sectors as a guest speaker.

Nádia Morais is a freelance linguist and writer. A bookworm and a polyglot, she has come to specialise in languages, journalism and strategic management. Currently, she mainly focuses on market analyses directed at the oil & gas and renewable energy market. She has published articles in Portugal, Germany, the UK and Angola. In parallel, she dedicates to translating from English, French and Spanish into Portuguese.

ENDNOTES

1 "Organization." Merriam-Webster. Merriam-Webster, n.d. Web. Jan. 2013..

2 "Economy." Merriam-Webster. Merriam-Webster, n.d. Web. Jan. 2013.

3 "Sustainable." Merriam-Webster. Merriam-Webster, n.d. Web. Jan. 2013.

4 "New Economy Definition | Investopedia." Investopedia. N.p., 24 Nov. 2003. Web. Jan. 2013.

5 "CRBiz Corporate Responsibility in Business." : Mahatma Gandhi: The Management Guru. N.p., n.d. Web. Feb. 2013.

6 "Leadership Lessons from Nelson Mandela." Future Builders. N.p., n.d. Web. Feb. 2013.

7 http://www.centstrat.com/wp-content/uploads/2010/07/leadership-lessons-from-mandela-1.pdf

8 Kraut, Richard. "Plato." Encyclopedia Britannica Online. Encyclopedia Britannica, n.d. Web. Feb. 2013.

9 Phillips, Christopher. Socrates Café: A Fresh Taste of Philosophy. New York: W.W. Norton, 2001. Print.

10 "Adam Smith: The Father Of Economics." Investopedia. N.p., 01 July 2008. Web. Feb. 2013..

11 "Wealth of Nations — Bk 1 Chpt 05." Wealth of Nations — Bk 1 Chpt 05. N.p., n.d. Web. Feb. 2013.

12 Crainer, Stuart. The Financial times Handbook of Management. London: FT/Pitman Pub., 1995. Print.

13 "Peter Drucker's Life and Legacy | The Drucker Institute." The Drucker Institute. N.p., n.d. Web. Apr. 2013.

14 http://science.howstuffworks.com/life/inside-the-mind/human-brain/brain3.htm

15 "Global Inequality | Inequality.org." Inequalityorg. N.p., n.d. Web. Apr. 2013.

16 "Lisdatacenter." Lisdatacenter Home Comments. N.p., n.d. Web. Apr. 2013.

17 "The World Top Incomes Database." The World Top Incomes Database. N.p., n.d. Web. Apr. 2013.

18 http://topincomes.g-mond.parisschoolofeconomics.eu/

19 "UNU-WIDER." UNU-WIDER : UNU-WIDER. N.p., n.d. Web. Apr. 2013.

20 https://www.oxfam.org/sites/www.oxfam.org/files/file_attachments/ib-wealth-having-all-wanting-more-190115-en.pdf

21 https://www.ecb.europa.eu/pub/pdf/scpwps/ecbwp1692.pdf

22 https://www.worldwealthreport.com/

23 http://www.wealthmanagement.ml.com/wm/pages/home.aspx

24 Global Wealth 2014: Riding a Wave of Growth

25 https://www.credit-suisse.com/ch/en/news-and-expertise/research/credit-suisse-

research-institute/publications.html

26 http://www.forbes.com/2011/03/08/world-billionaires-2011-intro.html

27 https://www.ted.com/speakers/james_b_glattfelder

28 http://arxiv.org/pdf/1107.5728.pdf

29 http://www.convergencealimentaire.info/map.jpg

30 http://english.pravda.ru/business/finance/18-10-2011/119355-The_Large_Families_that_rule_the_world-0/

31 http://dupress.com/articles/unlocking-the-passion-of-the-explorer/

32 http://www.worldheritage.org/articles/Gini_index

33 http://www.economist.com/news/briefing/21578643-world-has-astonishing-chance-take-billion-people-out-extreme-poverty-2030-not

34 http://www.worldwatch.org/

35 http://vitalsigns.worldwatch.org/vs-trend/wage-gap-widens-wages-fail-keep-pace-productivity

36 http://vitalsigns.worldwatch.org/sites/default/files/vital_signs_trend_final_pdf_global_wages.pdf

37 http://www.worldwatch.org/users/michael-renner

38 http://www.socialprogressimperative.org/data/spi

39 http://www.academia.edu/5433365/Joseph_Stiglitz_The_Price_of_Inequality

40 http://www.academia.edu/5433365/Joseph_Stiglitz_The_Price_of_Inequality

41 http://www.project-syndicate.org/commentary/the-instability-of-inequality

42 http://en.wikipedia.org/wiki/Gross_domestic_product

43 http://www.npr.org/blogs/money/2014/02/28/283477546/the-invention-of-the-economy

44 http://www.stiglitz-sen-fitoussi.fr/documents/rapport_anglais.pdf

45 http://aaseconomics.com/profile-dr-frank-shostak/

46 http://mises.org/daily/770

47 https://en.wikipedia.org/wiki/Simon_Kuznets

48 https://fraser.stlouisfed.org/scribd/?title_id=971&filepath=/docs/publications/natincome_1934/19340104_nationalinc.pdf

49 http://www.ft.com/intl/cms/s/2/dd2ec158-023d-11e4-ab5b-00144feab7de.html#axzz3IzMg8CEz

50 http://en.wikipedia.org/wiki/Zachary_Karabell

51 https://www.linkedin.com/pulse/20140305124209-3895280-forget-gdp-use-big-data?goback=%2Enmp_*1_*1_*1_*1_*1_*1_*1_*1_*1_*1&trk=nus-cha-roll-art-title

52 http://mgiep.unesco.org/wp-content/uploads/2014/12/IWR2014-WEB.pdf

53 https://drive.google.com/file/d/0B1bF9zth54L8SEliaF93ajJ2TUU/view?pli=1

54 http://www.jfklibrary.org/Research/Research-Aids/Ready-Reference/RFK-Speeches/Remarks-of-Robert-F-Kennedy-at-the-University-of-Kansas-March-18-1968.aspx

55 http://www.census.gov/newsroom/releases/archives/income_wealth/cb12-172.html

56 http://www.unicef.org/socialpolicy/files/Global_Inequality.pdf

57 http://www.telegraph.co.uk/finance/financetopics/davos/8283310/Davos-WEF-2011-Wealth-inequality-is-the-most-serious-challenge-for-the-world.html

58 http://www.ethicsandinternationalaffairs.org/2014/eliminating-extreme-inequality-a-sustainable-development-goal-2015-2030/

59 http://en.wikipedia.org/wiki/Gini_coefficient#Gini_coefficients_and_income_mobility

60 http://en.wikipedia.org/wiki/Anthony_Shorrocks#Shorrocks_index

61 http://www.grossnationalhappiness.com/

62 http://www.bhutanstudies.org.bt/

63 http://www.iim-edu.org/associates/medjones/

64 http://hdr.undp.org/en/content/human-development-index-hdi

65 http://www.payscale.com/

66 http://www.epi.org/publication/methodology-measuring-ceo-compensation-ratio/

67 https://www.capitaliq.com/home/what-we-offer/information-you-need/qualitative-data/execucomp.aspx

68 http://journals.cambridge.org/action/displayJournal?jid=EIA

69 http://www.stiglitz-sen-fitoussi.fr/documents/rapport_anglais.pdf

70 http://en.wikipedia.org/wiki/Income_inequality_metrics#Palma_ratio

71 http://senoreconorant.blogspot.pt/2011/09/guide-to-index-of-sustainable-economic.html

72 http://en.wikipedia.org/wiki/Income_inequality_metrics

73 http://www.neweconomics.org/

74 http://en.wikipedia.org/wiki/Gallup_%28company%29

75 http://en.wikipedia.org/wiki/Genuine_progress_indicator

76 http://genuineprogress.net/

77 http://hdr.undp.org/en/content/human-development-index-hdi

78 http://www.oecd.org/fr/social/yourbetterlifeindex.htm

79 http://www.sec.gov/investor/alerts/sayonpay.pdf

80 http://blogs.cfainstitute.org/marketintegrity/2013/12/26/say-on-pay-how-votes-on-executive-pay-is-evolving-globally-and-is-it-working/

81 http://www.businessdictionary.com/definition/bonus-malus-system.html

82 http://www.northeastern.edu/news/2013/11/paygapsproductivity/

83 http://www.forbes.com/sites/kathryndill/2014/04/15/report-ceos-earn-331-times-as-much-as-average-workers-774-times-as-much-as-minimum-wage-earners/

84 http://finance.yahoo.com/blogs/daily-ticker/ceos-more-350-times-average-worker-afl-cio-144537573.html

85 http://www.haygroup.com/downloads/uk/Getting-the-balance-right.pdf

86 http://www.sec.gov/about/laws/wallstreetreform-cpa.pdf

87 http://csrwiretalkback.tumblr.com/post/5371011123/ceo-worker-pay-ratio-rule-under-attack

88 http://www.aflcio.org/Corporate-Watch/Paywatch-2014

89 http://fr.workerscapital.org/connected/news/in-focus-afl-cio-white-paper-on-ceo-to-worker-pay-ratio-disclosure-and-its-importance-to-investors/

90 http://www.huffingtonpost.com/richard-trumka/

91 http://www.aflcio.org/Press-Room/Press-Releases/CEOs-Collect-Raises-Hoard-Record-Cash-Reserves

92 http://www.druckerinstitute.com/peter-druckers-life-and-legacy/

93 http://money.cnn.com/2012/08/20/investing/say-on-pay-citigroup/

94 http://csrwiretalkback.tumblr.com/post/5371011123/ceo-worker-pay-ratio-rule-under-attack

95 http://www.marketplace.org/topics/wealth-poverty/pay-day/some-companies-compare-and-cap-ceo-worker-pay-ratio

96 http://stats.oecd.org/Index.aspx?DataSetCode=IDD

97 http://www.actu.org.au/get-involved/current-campaigns

98 http://www.heritageinstitute.com/governance/compensation.htm

99 http://www.ons.gov.uk/ons/rel/ashe/annual-survey-of-hours-and-earnings/2012-provisional-results/stb-ashe-statistical-bulletin-2012.html

100 http://www.unia.ch/de/

101 http://www.swissinfo.ch/eng/wage-gap_salaries---the-great-social-and-moral-divide/34665536

102 http://www.kob.com/article/stories/s2654152.shtml

103 https://www.deco.proteste.pt/investe/20121119/772-Attach_s4983244.pdf

104 http://www.newsinenglish.no/2013/05/29/executive-pay-low-in-norway/

105 http://www.haygroup.com/se/press/details.aspx?id=36187

106 http://www.pwc.co.za/en_ZA/za/assets/pdf/executive-directors-report-2013.pdf

107 http://www.jplandman.co.za/Read.aspx?id=454

108 http://www.pecs.co.za/ceo-versus-staff-pay-gap-narrows.html

109 http://www.bloomberg.com/news/articles/2013-10-29/mining-ceo-pay-attacked-by-south-african-fund-managers

110 http://www.bloomberg.com/news/articles/2013-10-29/mining-ceo-pay-attacked-by-south-african-fund-managers

111 http://data.worldbank.org/indicator/SI.POV.GINI/countries?display=map

112 http://www.ibge.gov.br/english/

113 http://www.investopedia.com/terms/f/fractionalreservebanking.asp

114 http://en.wikipedia.org/wiki/Irving_Fisher

116 http://www.investopedia.com/terms/c/cartel.asp

117 http://www-personal.umich.edu/~maggiel/aba.pdf

118 http://topics.nytimes.com/top/reference/timestopics/subjects/h/high_frequency_algorithmic_trading/index.html

119 http://thedailyshow.cc.com/videos/3c1yvc/exclusive---joseph-stiglitz-extended-interview-pt--1

120 http://blog-imfdirect.imf.org/2011/03/25/observations-on-the-evolution-of-economic-policies/

121 http://blog-imfdirect.imf.org/2011/03/25/observations-on-the-evolution-of-economic-policies/

122 http://www.independent.co.uk/news/business/analysis-and-features/the-big-question-what-is-short-selling-and-is-it-a-practice-that-should-be-stamped-out-874717.html

123 http://opinionator.blogs.nytimes.com/2013/10/13/inequality-is-a-choice/?_php=true&_type=blogs&_r=1

124 http://cep.lse.ac.uk/piep/papers/Final_Report_V5.pdf

125 http://media.johnwiley.com.au/product_data/excerpt/71/07879556/0787955671.pdf

126 https://www.econ.berkeley.edu/sites/default/files/Soosun%20Tiah%20You_thesis.pdf

127 http://www.theatlantic.com/education/archive/2014/01/the-proven-way-to-fight-income-inequality-education/282875/

128 https://workingclassstudies.wordpress.com/2013/04/15/is-education-the-answer-to-economic-inequality/

129 http://www.ted.com/talks/dan_gilbert_asks_why_are_we_happy/transcript

131 http://en.wikipedia.org/wiki/Maslow's_hierarchy_of_needs

132 http://www-bcf.usc.edu/~easterl/papers/Happiness.pdf

133 http://ineteconomics.org/people/robert-skidelsky

134 http://en.chessbase.com/post/skidelsky-how-much-is-enough-

135 http://www.brookings.edu/research/papers/2013/04/subjective-well-being-income

136 http://www.pnas.org/content/107/38/16489.full

137 http://news.stanford.edu/news/2010/january25/money-happiness-research-012210.html

138 http://www.pnas.org/content/107/38/16489.full

139 http://www.nytimes.com/2015/04/14/business/owner-of-gravity-payments-a-credit-card-processor-is-setting-a-new-minimum-wage-70000-a-year.html?smprod=nytcore-iphone&smid=nytcore-iphone-share&_r=1

140 http://www.ons.gov.uk/ons/dcp171778_385428.pdf

141 http://www.ncbi.nlm.nih.gov/pmc/articles/PMC2944762/

142 Piketty, Thomas (2013) Capital in the Twenty-first Century. Cambridge, MA: Harvard University Press.

143 http://crowdsourcing.typepad.com/cs/2006/06/crowdsourcing_a.html

144 http://www.crowdsourcingverband.de/wp-content/uploads/2013/01/Brabham_Crowdsourcing_Problem_Solving.pdf

145 http://www.wikipedia.org/

146 https://www.kickstarter.com/

147 https://www.indiegogo.com/

148 http://www.rockethub.com/

149 http://www.gofundme.com/

150 http://www.razoo.com/

151 https://www.coursera.org/

152 https://www.udacity.com/

153 https://www.edx.org/

154 http://www.obhe.ac.uk/newsletters/borderless_report_october_2012/are_moocs_a_game_changer_for_higher_education

155 http://p2pfoundation.net/P2P_Currency

156 https://www.youtube.com/watch?v=jhgoTs2mOg8

157 https://www.youtube.com/watch?v=vqmTgyrOquQ

158 http://www.positivemoney.org/

159 http://openmoney.org/

160 https://bitcoin.org/en/

161 The 'Ponzi Scheme' is named after Charles Ponzi, a clerk in Boston who first orchestrated such a scheme in 1919. It is a fraudulent investing scam that promises high rates of return with little risk to investors. It works by generating returns for older investors by acquiring new investors and yields the promised returns as long as there are more new investors. Usually, these schemes end up collapsing when the new investment

stops. *In* http://www.investopedia.com/terms/p/ponzischeme.asp

162 http://p2pfoundation.net/P2P_Currency_Systems

163 http://money.cnn.com/galleries/2012/pf/1201/gallery.community-currencies/6.html

164 http://money.cnn.com/galleries/2012/pf/1201/gallery.community-currencies/6.html

165 http://hbswk.hbs.edu/item/7045.html

166 http://hbswk.hbs.edu/item/7704.html

167 http://www.inc.com/chuck-blakeman/marissa-mayer-the-old-school-manager-vs-ricardo-semler-the-participation-age-lea.html

168 http://en.wikipedia.org/wiki/Wage_slavery

169 http://www.themaritzinstitute.com/~/media/Files/MaritzInstitute/White-Papers/Employee-Enrichment-A-New-Imperative-The-Maritz-Institute.pdf

170 http://www.campuscareercenter.com/full_jobs/2655549/Deloitte/Future_Leaders_Apprentice_Program_FLAP_.html

171 http://www.fastcompany.com/3004953/how-sas-became-worlds-best-place-work

172 http://tibettalk.wordpress.com/2010/05/23/the-hierarchy-of-tibetan-buddhism/

173 http://planksandnails.hubpages.com/hub/-Hierarchical-Structure-in-the-Modern-Church

174 Kenneth Meyer, author of the book Pull Thinking®: Harness the Power of Pull to Fuel Growth and Ignite Performance by Aligning People, Culture and Purpose

175 http://www.scientificamerican.com/article/to-trust-or-not-to-trust/

176 http://c.ymcdn.com/sites/www.istr.org/resource/resmgr/working_papers_toronto/diniz.lisa.pdf

177 http://www.marketwatch.com/story/rios-carnival-not-just-a-local-party-anymore-2012-02-13?pagenumber=2

178 Filho, Luiz Carlos Prestes (2009) *Cadeia Produtiva da Economia do Carnaval.* Editora E-papers

179 http://ledna.org/sites/ledna.org/files/generating_economic_opportunities_through_street_carnivals.pdf

180 http://haas.berkeley.edu/faculty/papers/anderson/functions%20and%20dysfunctions%20of%20hierarchy.pdf

181 Mackenzie, Kenneth D. (1991) *The Organizational Hologram: The Effective Management of Organizational Change.* Springer Science & Business Media.

182 http://99u.com/articles/22853/do-we-really-need-managers?utm_source=Triggermail&utm_medium=email&utm_term=ALL&utm_campaign=MIH%20-%20Mar%20%2714

183 Zander, Benjamin & Zander, Rosamund Stone (2002) The Art of Possibility: Transforming Professional and Personal Life: Penguin Books.

184 http://www.wholesomewords.org/missions/bliving21.html

185 http://knowledge.wharton.upenn.edu/article/mercenaries-vs-missionaries-john-doerr-sees-two-kinds-of-internet-entrepreneurs/

186 http://ecorner.stanford.edu/authorMaterialInfo.html?mid=1274

187 Ricci, Ron and Wiese,Carl. (2011) The Collaboration Imperative: Executive Strategies for Unlocking Your Organisation's True Potential. Cisto Systems.

188 http://www.asaecenter.org/Resources/EUArticle.cfm?ItemNumber=11786

189 http://www.fastcompany.com/3044963/hit-the-ground-running/the-key-to-creating-socially-conscious-businesses

190 http://www.mckinsey.com/insights/organization/the_ceos_role_in_leading_transformation

191 http://www.leadershipnow.com/CoveyOnTrust.html

192 Sprenger, Reinhard K. (2007) Trust: The Best Way to Manage: Campus Verlag

193 http://oss-watch.ac.uk/resources/meritocraticgovernancemodel

194 http://www.ncsociology.org/sociationtoday/v21/merit.htm

195 http://digitalcommons.ilr.cornell.edu/cgi/viewcontent.cgi?article=1106&context=cahrswp

196 http://www.newyorker.com/magazine/2010/10/11/talent-grab

197 http://knowledge.wharton.upenn.edu/article/outrage-over-outsized-executive-compensation-who-should-fix-it-and-how/

198 https://www.linkedin.com/pulse/20141104162446-2459096-is-the-world-s-most-secretive-company-opening-up

199 Tapscott, Don. (1997) The Digital Economy: Promise and Peril in the Age of Networked Intelligence. McGraw-Hill.

200 http://knowledge.wharton.upenn.edu/article/everything-from-oil-to-silver-are-speculators-causing-too-much-volatility/

201 http://www.centstrat.com/wp-content/uploads/2010/07/leadership-lessons-from-mandela-1.pdf

202 A Taxonomy of Organizational Justice Theories. Jerald Greenberg. The Academy of Management Review, Vol. 12, No. 1. (Jan., 1987), pp. 9-22.

203 "Creating Shared Value." Harvard Business Review. N.p., 01 Jan. 2011. Web. Dec. 2014. https://hbr.org/2011/01/the-big-idea-creating-shared-value

204 http://www.sustainablemeasures.com/node/89

205 As suggested by Peter Drucker

206 For this example we considered that all the revenues come from barrels of oil

207 http://www.americansfortaxfairness.org/files/Walmart-on-Tax-Day-Americans-for-Tax-Fairness-1.pdf

208 http://www.smithsonianmag.com/smart-news/how-much-is-wikipedia-worth-704865/?no-ist

209 http://gondwanaland.com/mlog/2013/10/08/wikipedias-economic-values/

210 http://www.britannica.com/EBchecked/topic/505662/Robin-Hood